Praise for *Near-Death Experiences*

"Scott Smith has researched and written a very interesting book about the intriguing topic of near-death experiences—from a Catholic perspective. The insights, examples, and witnesses he provides of near-death experiences from Sacred Scripture, papal writings, lives of the saints, and Catholics from all walks of life—as well as what modern medical research has to say on the subject—make for a truly fascinating read!"

—Fr. Donald Calloway, M.I.C.
Author, *No Turning Back: A Witness to Mercy*

"Scott Smith's *Near-Death Experiences* is a spiritually sobering book. Smith piques the Catholic reader's interest in the Four Last Things—Death, Judgment, Heaven, and Hell—through the lens of near-death experiences. A well-researched work with true stories from Scripture and the saints. You won't be able to put this book down!"

—Patrick O'Hearn
Author, *Our Lady of Sorrows*

NEAR-DEATH EXPERIENCES

Scott L. Smith, Jr.

NEAR-DEATH EXPERIENCES

SOPHIA INSTITUTE PRESS
Manchester, New Hampshire

Sophia Institute Press
Box 5284, Manchester, NH 03108
1-800-888-9344

www.SophiaInstitute.com

Sophia Institute Press® is a registered trademark of Sophia Institute.

hardcover ISBN 979-8-88911-114-6

ebook ISBN 979-8-88911-115-3

Library of Congress Control Number: 2024952238

Second printing

CONTENTS

NEAR-DEATH EXPERIENCES

INTRODUCTION

They should have sent a poet.

By now, I must have researched or interviewed people regarding hundreds of accounts of near-death experiences (NDE). In all of these interviews, I have always been struck by the same thing: Those who have been to the doorstep of eternity invariably struggle to find the words to describe adequately their experience.

One of these individuals, Fr. Cedric Pisegna, puts it well: "I'm trying to describe the most dramatic, traumatic moment of my life, but words do not suffice."

Words would, of course, be a problem. These people are encountering the supernatural—and many of them, in one form or another, are meeting *God Himself*: God, the Creator of worlds and words. God's Son is *the* Word. How could any post-Fall, post-Babel, post-Flood language adequately describe this experience?

That's why I'm reminded of Dr. Eleanor "Ellie" Arroway's line from the movie adaptation of Carl Sagan's book *Contact*: "*They should have sent a poet.*"

Ellie says these words as she is witnessing the greatest galactic sight in human history, a sight that defies description—except by poets and believers.

Sadly, Carl Sagan was an atheist, so the greatest thing he could imagine was still mired in the material world. Nevertheless, he accurately indicates the paltriness of words when describing the transcendently and immanently good, true, and beautiful.

Sagan's words seem to echo St. Paul's: "What no eye has seen, nor ear heard, nor the heart of man conceived, what God has prepared for those who love him" (1 Cor. 2:9). May the Holy Spirit enlighten your minds, so that what you read will be far greater than my words.

Finding Catholicism

Do you know how, when you've found a fascinating topic, it doesn't just go deeper and deeper? It gets bigger and bigger the deeper you go. Catholicism surpasses all other fields, topics, subjects, and sects in this regard.

G. K. Chesterton relates this aspect of the Church to an encounter he had with the Crystal Palace in his youth. The Crystal Palace was a massive cast-iron and glass structure originally erected in London's Hyde Park to house the Great Exhibition of 1851. Conceived by Prince Albert, the Great Exhibition showcased the vastness of the British Empire's ideas and products from its territories, provinces, colonies, and holdings all over the world. Chesterton wrote the following analogy about this structure:

> Every man conceives himself as moving about in a cosmos of some kind; and the man of the days of my youth walked about in a kind of vast and airy Crystal Palace in which there were exhibits set side by side. The cosmos, being made of glass and iron, was partly transparent and partly colorless; anyhow, there was something negative about it; arching over all our heads, a roof as remote as a sky, it seemed to be impartial and impersonal. Our attention was fixed on the exhibits, which were all carefully ticketed and arranged

in rows; for it was the age of science. Here stood all the religions in a row—the churches or sects or whatever we called them; and towards the end of the row there was a particularly dingy and dismal one, with a pointed roof half fallen in and pointed windows most broken with stones by passers-by; and we were told that this particular exhibit was the Roman Catholic Church. Some of us were sorry for it and even fancied it had been rather badly used; most of us regarded it as dirty and disreputable; a few of us even pointed out that many details in the ruin were artistically beautiful or architecturally important. But most people preferred to deal at other and more business-like booths at the Quaker shop of Peace and Plenty or the Salvation Army store where the showman beats the big drum outside.[1]

He describes the Catholic Church as—at first glance and first thought—appearing as just one religion among many. It is just one dingy exhibit in the Crystal Palace beside much shinier and louder exhibits, while the showmen are beating their drums, distracting us from the sad, forgotten Catholic exhibit. But this first impression is not accurate, for Chesterton continues (emphasis added): "Conversion consists very largely, on its intellectual side, in the discovery that all that picture of equal creeds inside an indifferent cosmos is quite false. It is not a question of comparing the merits and defects of the Quaker meeting-house set beside the Catholic cathedral. It is the Quaker meeting-house that is *inside* the Catholic cathedral; *it is the Catholic cathedral that covers everything like the vault of the Crystal Palace.*"[2]

---

[1] G. K. Chesterton, *The Catholic Church and Conversion* (New York: Macmillan, 1926), 29.

[2] Chesterton, *Church and Conversion*, 29.

The Catholic Church is not one exhibit among many others lining the aisles of the Crystal Palace; the Church *is* the Crystal Palace, in her entirety, and she is far more: She is the cosmos itself. This realization, Chesterton says, is the substance of intellectual conversion.

When I was a younger man, I tried on many different philosophical hats. I remember being fascinated by Ayn Rand, the author of *Atlas Shrugged* and *The Fountainhead*. I had never read anything like those novels before, and I went all in. From there, I read everything Rand had ever written. I fully embraced the ideas of her philosophy, called "objectivism." It was a rejection of the Marxism—the "collectivism," as she called it—of Soviet communism.

Rand spoke what seemed to be marvelous truths and told gripping stories. I savored what I experienced through her as novel, visceral truth. But Rand was also an atheist—an unfortunate side effect of Soviet Marxism. I realized that, as I dug deeper and deeper into Ayn Rand, I found less and less. The deeper I studied, the smaller her ideas became. The original savor of what I thought was truth grew less and less. I realized that it was fleeting—and then, all at once, it was gone.

But with Catholicism, I have had the completely opposite experience. The more I discover, the more I see there is to discover. This, I think, is the foretaste of Heaven that the Church, unique among all institutions of world history and all the exhibits of the Crystal Palace, is able to offer us.

This is also the way that C. S. Lewis described Heaven in the last (and my favorite) of his Chronicles of Narnia. In *The Last Battle*, the unicorn captures everyone's experience of Aslan's country, or Heaven: "I have come home at last! This is my real country! I belong here. This is the land I have been looking for all my life, though I never knew it till now.... Come further up, come further in!"[3]

Heaven is the ascent up the mountain in *The Last Battle*. The "further up" and "further in" you go, the bigger it becomes. This is true in every sphere of Catholicism that I have studied, and here, for our present purposes, I also discovered that it is certainly true in the realm of near-death experiences (NDEs). As we focus in on the subject of this book, let's take a look at what that means.

What Is a Catholic Near-Death Experience?

As you might imagine, there is some disagreement and some gray area as to what actually constitutes an NDE, but I will make sure to provide you with the appropriate classification wherever possible.

This book was born of an odd genesis. A nondenominational friend, Shaun Tabatt, suggested that I write specifically on Catholic NDEs.[4] At the time, I wasn't even sure I believed in them. But once I had committed to writing this book, I asked God for help. God would have to provide, if this book was His will. And God surprised me by responding to my presumption with a fire hose. Suddenly, the stories and reports of NDEs were everywhere. This pocket of the universe had suddenly opened up to me.

---

[3] C. S. Lewis, *The Last Battle* (New York: HarperTrophy, 2000), 195–197.

[4] Shaun Tabatt has published two books of contemporary accounts of NDEs: *Near Death Experiences: 101 Short Stories That Will Help You Understand Heaven, Hell, and the Afterlife* (2023) and *Real Near Death Experience Stories: True Accounts of Those Who Died and Experienced Immortality* (2022).

Shaun had noticed something. No books on NDEs from a uniquely Catholic perspective existed; there were some personal memoirs, such as Fr. Cedric Pisegna's, which I'll share with you in part 3, but there was nothing *comprehensive*.

Then I began to wonder: What makes a near-death experience uniquely *Catholic*? Perhaps it is the involvement of the Virgin Mary and other saints—that would be a good start. Once I began thinking about it, trying to puzzle it out, I realized there was a treasure trove of uniquely Catholic stories just waiting to be told. And, the thing is, as Catholics, we don't have merely contemporary accounts; we have *millennia*. We have a rich history, thousands of years of amazing stories of NDEs to tell. I'm excited to share some of these stories with you, so that your faith will be strengthened and so that you will become evangelizers of *the realities of Heaven, Hell, and Purgatory.*

Near-Death Experiences versus Out-of-Body Experiences

Before we dig into thousands of years of Catholic NDEs—as experienced by saints, priests, and popes—it is important to make some distinctions. This can be confusing business!

Some accounts in this book will not technically be NDEs but will be similar to them. A Catholic NDE is a subjective supernatural experience involving an encounter with the Divine that is triggered by a life-threatening situation. We will refer to them as out-of-body experiences (OBEs). For example, St. John's experience, as described in the book of Revelation, was not, as far as we know, an NDE. But we can safely demonstrate from Scripture that St. John's experience was an OBE. We can suggest more only through speculation. Certain theories are possible or even plausible but not clearly demonstrable.

So what's the difference between an OBE and an NDE? An OBE is a conscious feeling of being separated from the body. Fr. Cedric Pisegna's OBE, discussed later in this book, was not triggered by a life-threatening situation. He was just watching a Boston Red Sox game—though being a Red Sox fan back then could have been a harrowing experience!

Here's what can get confusing. OBEs are a common characteristic of NDEs; nearly half of the people who have had an NDE also reported an OBE.[5] During an OBE, people may feel elevated and have some spatial awareness. They may see and hear events happening on earth from a perspective outside their bodies. NDEs, however, also typically include other experiences, such as seeing a light, a tunnel, or a deceased family member, or feeling intense emotions. These characteristics, particular to NDEs, will be described in greater depth below.

NDEs appear to be a global phenomenon, an experience common to all mankind, to human nature itself, if not to every individual. They have been reported by children, adults, scientists, physicians, priests, ministers, the religious, and atheists from countries around the world. They have been reported by about 17 percent of those who experience an injury that brings them close to death—or to death itself.[6]

---

[5] Olaf Blanke, Nathan Faivre, Sebastian Dieguez, "Leaving Body and Life Behind: Out-of-Body and Near-Death Experience," in *The Neurology of Consciousness*, ed. Steven Laureys, Olivia Gosseries, and Giulio Tononi, 2nd ed. (Amsterdam: Academic Press, 2016), 323–347.

[6] N. L. Zingrone and C. S. Alvarado, "Pleasurable Western Adult Near-Death Experiences: Features, Circumstances, and Incidence," in *The Handbook of Near-Death Experiences: Thirty Years of Investigation*, ed. J. M. Holden, B. Greyson, and D. James (Santa Barbara, CA: Praeger/ABC-CLIO, 2009), 17–40.

No two NDEs are the same. Nevertheless, there are characteristic features that are commonly observed across the spectrum of NDEs. Medical researchers have identified several common characteristics of NDEs, which I have modified slightly:[7]

- Disembodiment: a perception of seeing and hearing apart from the physical body (the OBE portion of an NDE)
- Tunnel experience: passing into or through a tunnel
- Intense light: encountering a mystical light
- Joy: intense and generally positive emotions
- Life review: a review of part or all of their prior life experiences
- Encounter: meeting and encountering deceased loved ones, saints, or even the Divine
- Decision: a choice to return to earthly life

I have found that the "tunnel experience" is a relatively recent characteristic of NDEs. However, something analogous to this tunnel experience, this feeling of being physically transported, has been documented since antiquity. It has been variously described as a sense of soaring or flight, being "caught up," as St. Paul described it, or "flung" out of one's body.

Medical Research into Near-Death Experiences

Faith and reason are like two wings on which the human spirit rises to the contemplation of truth; and God has placed in the human heart a desire to know the truth—in a word, to know himself—so that, by knowing and loving

---

[7] Jeffrey Long, M.D., "Near-Death Experience: Evidence for Their Reality," *Missouri Medicine* 111, no. 5 (September–October 2014): 372–380.

God, men and women may also come to the fullness of truth about themselves. (Pope St. John Paul II, *Fides et Ratio*)

The most beautiful and most profound experience is the sensation of the mystical. It is the sower of all true science. (Albert Einstein, *The Merging of Spirit and Science*)

The mainstream medical world firmly denounces the phenomenon of NDEs; much less does it attribute any supernatural significance to them. And that is consistent with the mainstream assumptions of our modern world, afflicted as it is with hyper-empiricism and ultra-materialism: if it can't be proven in a test tube or a Petri dish, it's not real. It's not *truth*.

But this is a self-contradicting mindset. These same scientists who say a belief must be based on empirical evidence dogmatically assert, without evidence, that all supernatural phenomenon is false, bogus, or, at best, a hallucination.

But what if these scientists and doctors used the scientific method to study and analyze NDEs? What amazing insights into the nature of human consciousness, the soul, and the afterlife could be found, if people looked at these phenomena *scientifically*? That is, what if scientists didn't start with the unscientific assumption, the axiom, that all supernatural phenomenon is hogwash? What could we discover *then*?

Thankfully, there are a number of respected medical researchers, doctors, and scientists who believe in NDEs, or at least who can no longer, in good conscience, deny them. In fact, extensive medical research has been conducted on both NDEs and OBEs. While the focus of this book will be specifically on Catholic NDEs and OBEs, let's get started by taking a look at some of this research into NDEs across the board.

AWARE Study

One of the most comprehensive and well-known medical studies of NDEs is the AWARE study, led by Dr. Sam Parnia.[8] He was joined by doctors and researchers and by representatives from hospitals in and around London, across the United Kingdom and Europe, and in the United States.[9] Phase one of their four-year study ended in 2012. Of 2,060 people who suffered cardiac arrest and clinical death at the participating hospitals, 16 percent were resuscitated and survived, at least until the point of discharge from the hospitals. Of the 330 survivors, 101 patients were found eligible for inclusion in the study, consented to it, and fully completed the interview process.

The researchers conducted a three-stage interview of these 101 eligible survivors. Of the 101, nine experienced NDEs—that's about 9 percent of survivors. Of these nine, only two had audio

[8] S. Parnia et al., "AWARE—AWAreness during REsuscitation—a Prospective Study," *Resuscitation* 85, no. 12 (2014), doi: 10.1016/j.resuscitation.2014.09.004.

[9] Stony Brook Medical Center, State University of New York at Stony Brook, New York, USA; Hammersmith Hospital Imperial College, University of London, UK; Montefiore Medical Center, New York, USA; University Hospital Southampton, Southampton, UK; Royal Bournemouth Hospital, Bournemouth, UK; St Georges Hospital, University of London, UK; Emory University School of Medicine and Atlanta Veterans Affairs Medical Center, Atlanta, USA; Medical University of Vienna, Austria; Northampton General Hospital, Northampton, UK; Lister Hospital, Stevenage, UK; Cedar Sinai, USA; Croydon University Hospital, UK; James Paget Hospital, UK; Ashford and St Peters NHS Trust, UK; Addenbrookes Hospital, University of Cambridge, UK; East Sussex Hospital, East Sussex, UK; Indiana University, Wishard Memorial Hospital, Indianapolis, USA; and University of Virginia, Charlottesville, Virginia, USA.

and visual awareness of what they had experienced and could also later recall what had happened.

One of these survivors, a fifty-seven-year-old man, recalled observing events from an upper corner of the room that he was lying in. He accurately described people who were present and sounds and activities that occurred during his resuscitation; everything he described was corroborated by his medical records, specifically the use of an automated external defibrillator.

Here are some excerpts from his interviews with the researchers (emphasis added):

> I have come back from the other side of life.... God sent me back, it was not my time—I had many things to do.... I traveled through a tunnel toward a very strong light, which didn't dazzle or hurt my eyes.... There were other people in the tunnel whom I did not recognize. When I emerged, I described a very beautiful crystal city.... There was *a river that ran through the middle of the city with the most crystal-clear waters.* There were many people, without faces, who were washing in the waters.... The people were very beautiful.... There was the most beautiful singing ... and I was moved to tears. My next recollection was looking up at a doctor doing chest compressions.[10]

Does this description of Heaven sound familiar? In Revelation 22:1–2, the angel took the apostle John on a tour of the heavenly city. Look at how similar St. John's account is to this man's: "Then he showed me the river of the water of life, bright as crystal, flowing from the throne of God and of the Lamb through the middle of the street of the city."

[10] Parnia, "AWARE," table 2.

But I am getting ahead of myself. As you will see, the first part of this book discusses examples of NDEs from the Bible; we will talk more about the experiences of John and other biblical figures in those first three chapters.

More Medical Research into NDE Phenomena

In addition to the work of Dr. Sam Parnia and his colleagues, a surprising amount of medical and scientific research has been conducted in the field of NDEs. The following is a brief survey of large-scale, credible medical studies of the NDE phenomenon.

Since the early 1970s, there have been a number of retrospective and prospective studies of cardiac arrest in which patients' experiences, including NDEs, have been examined.[11] The common characteristics of these NDEs, at least those that were studied, were (1) coming to a border of no return, (2) feeling peace, (3) feeling joy, (4) seeing a bright light, (5) losing awareness of one's body, and (6) seeing deceased relatives. These early studies involved small population sizes, and there were no reports of watching resuscitation staff from above or recalling specific details of cardiac arrest resuscitation procedures.[12]

A large Dutch study of 344 cardiac arrest survivors from ten hospitals was published in 2001. Respondents were interviewed over a two-year period, and forty-one (12 percent) of the survivors

[11] R. L. White and S. C. Liddon, "Ten Survivors of Cardiac Arrest," *Psychiatry Medicine* 3, no. 3 (1972): 219–225; S. B. Schoenbeck and G. D. Hocutt, "Near-Death Experiences in Patients Undergoing Cardiopulmonary Resuscitation," *Journal of Near-Death Studies* 9 (1991): 211–218.

[12] S. Parnia et al., "Near Death Experiences, Cognitive Function and Psychological Outcomes of Surviving Cardiac Arrest," *Resuscitation* (2007), doi:10.1016/j.resuscitation.2007.01.020.

reported similar experiences to those described above.[13] Also, unlike the participants in the studies summarized in the paragraph immediately above, 24 percent of those who experienced an NDE in this 2001 study also reported being able to watch and remember specific events from their cardiac arrest.

In one interesting case, a nurse reported having removed a patient's dentures and placed them in a drawer in a special crash trolley. This happened while the patient was in a coma, in which he remained through the one and a half hours of his resuscitation.

One week later, the patient returned to the same ward and, upon seeing the nurse, said, "Oh, that nurse knows where my dentures are." The patient went on to describe exactly how the nurse had removed his dentures and put them into the crash trolley.

The patient also added specific details about the trolley: "It had all these bottles on it, and there was this sliding drawer underneath, and that's where you put my teeth."

The nurse's response to this strange occurrence was also documented:

I was especially amazed because I remembered this happening while the man was in a deep coma and in the process of CPR. When asked further, it appeared that the man had seen himself lying in bed and that he had perceived from above how the nurses and doctors had been busy with CPR. He had also been able to describe correctly and in detail the small room in which he had been resuscitated as well as the appearance of those present.

[13] P. van Lommel, R. van Wees, V. Meyers, and I. Elfferich, "Near-Death Experience in Survivors of Cardiac Arrest: A Prospective Study in The Netherlands," *Lancet* 358, no. 9298 (2001): 2039–2045.

It is incredible to find such documentation of seemingly supernatural phenomenon in medical studies. It is fortunate that the researchers chronicled this exchange between the patient and his nurse. It makes one wonder how often such details are left undocumented and unverified.

Two American studies of NDEs in cardiac arrest were also published in the early 2000s. One study of nearly sixteen hundred cardiac patients over a thirty-month period found that the incidence of NDEs increased with the severity of the cardiac disease. Only 1 percent of those admitted with stable cardiac disease reported NDEs. This increased to 10 percent of those who were admitted with cardiac arrest.[14] The second U.S. study found that 23 percent of cardiac arrest survivors had had an NDE. This second study further found, in following up with patients within six months of their NDEs, that they were positively transformed by having had an NDE.[15] In general and across multiple studies, patients with NDEs were subsequently found to be happier, more socially orientated, less materialistic, more altruistic, and less afraid of death than people who had not had such an experience.[16]

Overall, the quantity of credible medical research into NDE phenomenon has been steadily increasing since the 1970s. These studies are all captivating and worthy of further examination; winnowing their results to just the few that we've looked at here was a challenging exercise! But hopefully this cursory examination of

[14] B. Greyson, "Incidence and Correlates of Near-Death Experiences in a Cardiac Care Unit," *General Hospital Psychiatry* 25, no. 4 (2003): 269–276.

[15] J. Schwaninger, "A Prospective Analysis of Near-Death Experiences in Cardiac Arrest Patients," *Journal of Near-Death Experiences* 20, no. 4 (2002).

[16] Parnia, "Near Death Experiences."

decades of excellent research has provided you with a good foundation for the rest of our discussions in this book.

Now that we have established some terminology and common characteristics of NDEs, at least for contemporaneous accounts, let's dig into some of the biblical and historical accounts of these phenomena to get a better understanding of specifically Catholic NDEs and OBEs.

Part I

NEAR-DEATH EXPERIENCES IN THE BIBLE

To paraphrase Marcel Proust, real discovery consists not in seeing new sights but in looking with new eyes. With that in mind, I'm about to take some familiar stories from the Bible and make them seem very unfamiliar.[17]

Many overlooked NDEs and OBEs occur in the Bible. You might hear people remark, as I did before undertaking this project, something to the effect of, "Oh, I never thought about that being an NDE." But once you begin to accept these experiences as just a category of man's spiritual and religious experiences with God, you return to the Bible with a fresh set of eyes. You start to see them throughout Scripture.

Where? Everywhere.

---

[17] Here is the quotation: "The only true voyage of discovery, the only fountain of Eternal Youth, would be not to visit strange lands but to possess other eyes, to behold the universe through the eyes of another, of a hundred others, to behold the hundred universes that each of them beholds, that each of them is; and this we can contrive with an Elstir, with a Vinteuil; with men like these we do really fly from star to star." Marcel Proust, *The Captive*, vol. 5 of *Remembrance of Things Past.*

You begin to ask questions like these:

Was the entire book of Revelation an account of the apostle John's NDE or, perhaps more accurately, an OBE?

When Moses went up Mount Sinai, into the glory cloud of fire and lightning, and saw Heaven—after Aaron and the Israelites had assumed he was dead—was that an NDE?

Did *all* the prophets have NDEs or OBEs? Take one of Daniel's prophetic visions, for example. Many NDEs and OBES, like that of Fr. Cedric Pisegna, whose NDE will be described in part 3 of this book, take the form of the vision that the prophet Daniel had "as he lay in his bed" (Dan. 7:1). The typical experience of encountering a "being of light" of "infinite love" is understood to be God the Father—is that so different from what Daniel saw? "As I looked, thrones were placed and one that was ancient of days took his seat; his raiment was white as snow, and the hair of his head like pure wool; his throne was fiery flames, its wheels were burning fire" (Dan. 7:9).

And surely the account of the Transfiguration has details in it that sound like many documented accounts of NDEs:

And as he was praying, the appearance of his countenance was altered, and his raiment became dazzling white. And behold, two men talked with him, Moses and Elijah, who appeared in glory and spoke of his departure, which he was to accomplish at Jerusalem. Now Peter and those who were with him were heavy with sleep but kept awake, and they saw his glory and the two men who stood with him. (Luke 9:29–32)

These biblical encounters closely match the characteristics of NDEs seen today. The difference? The biblical NDE and OBE accounts are *canonical*—that is, trustworthy and credible beyond all doubt.

We can think on these things with even more clarity when we look at the biblical stories in which people actually died and then came back. All those who experienced being raised from the dead—such as Lazarus, Jairus's daughter, and the son of the widow of Nain—what did they see? And what about Jonah and St. Paul?

Those last two might surprise you. Were St. Paul and Jonah really two of the biblical figures who were raised from the dead? Let's dig into these biblical passages together to see what we can find out.

1

JONAH: NOT JUST IN THE BELLY OF A WHALE

The Sign of Jonah

Jonah was swallowed into the belly of a whale, right? He was spat onto the shore after three days in that belly, but he was alive the whole time. Wasn't he? *Wasn't* he?

Actually, no. He wasn't.

Do you remember Jesus' mysterious prophecy about the "Sign of Jonah"? Here is Luke 11:29–32 (emphasis added):

When the crowds were increasing, he began to say, "This generation is an evil generation; it seeks a sign, but no sign shall be given to it except the sign of Jonah. *For as Jonah became a sign to the men of Nineveh, so will the Son of man be to this generation.* The queen of the South will arise at the judgment with the men of this generation and condemn them; for she came from the ends of the earth to hear the wisdom of Solomon, and behold, something greater than Solomon is here. The men of Nineveh will arise at the judgment with this generation and condemn it; for they repented at the preaching of Jonah, and behold, *something greater than Jonah* is here.

"Jonah became a sign to the men of Nineveh." "So will the Son of man be to this generation." Jesus is the Son of man, but Jesus is never swallowed by a whale (or a great fish). How, then, does Jesus provide the sign of Jonah?

This is a confusing passage. When you first read it, it may seem like Jesus is being flippant or evasive. However, there are no empty phrases in Scripture. So we have to ask ourselves: What is the deeper meaning of the sign of Jonah? What does Jesus mean by referring to it?

First, we can consider that Jonah was in the belly of the whale for three days, while Jesus was in the belly of the earth for three days. Are, then, those three days after being "swallowed" that they have in common what Jesus means by "the sign of Jonah"? This is getting us closer, but there's more.

Let's look at the text of the book of Jonah, specifically at Jonah 2:2–9. This is Jonah's prayer to the Lord, his cry for help (emphasis added):

> I called to the LORD, out of my distress and He answered me; out of the belly of Sheol I cried, and thou didst hear my voice. For thou didst cast me into the deep, into the heart of the seas, and the flood was round about me; all thy waves and thy billows passed over me. Then I said, "I am cast out from thy presence; how shall I again look upon holy temple?" The waters closed in over me, *the deep was round about me, weeds were wrapped about my head at the roots of the mountains.* I went down to the land whose bars closed upon me for ever; yet *thou didst bring up my life from the Pit,* O LORD my God. When my soul fainted within me, I remembered the LORD; and my prayer came to thee, into thy holy temple. Those who pay regard to vain idols forsake

their true loyalty. But I with the voice of thanksgiving will sacrifice to thee; what I have vowed I will pay. Deliverance belongs to the LORD!

Notice that Jonah is crying for help from the belly of Sheol, also sometimes translated as the "depths of Sheol"—not from the depths of the ocean or even the depths of a fish. Jonah is crying to God from Sheol—which is the abode of the *dead.*

Also, Jonah says that God has brought up his life from the *pit.* This is another Old Testament term for the realm of the dead.[18]

Jonah sinks down below the "weeds," the "roots of the mountains," and is engulfed by the great deep. Jonah's soul is descending to the bottom of the ocean—and even deeper than that. He sinks below the depths of the oceans, deep into the earth, far past the belly of any fish or whale.

Add to this that the trip to the underworld land of the dead was generally believed in the Near East to be a journey of *three days,*[19] and we come to a simple conclusion: Jonah died. Jonah was *dead.*

One of the early Christian writers attests to Jonah's death as well. Tertullian references the case of Jonah to illustrate God's divine power of restoring the dead to life, whatever disaster may have befallen them: "Now I apprehend that in the case of Jonah we

---

[18] Brant Pitre, *The Case for Jesus: The Biblical and Historical Evidence for Christ* (New York: Image Books, 2016), 150–152: "Belly of Sheol" and "the pit" are Old Testament terms that refer to the realm of the dead (see Job 7:9; 33:18; Ps. 40:2; 49:14–15; 89:48).

[19] See Robert Chisholm, *Handbook on the Prophets* (Grand Rapids, MI: Baker Academic, 2002), 411: "In ancient Near Eastern literature, the trip to the underworld land of the dead was viewed as a three-day journey." See also George M. Landes, "The 'Three Days and Three Nights' Motif in Jonah 2:1," *Journal of Biblical Literature* 86 (1967): 246–250.

have a fair proof of this divine power, when he comes forth from the fish's belly uninjured in both his natures—his flesh and his soul. No doubt the bowels of the whale would have had abundant time during three days for consuming and digesting Jonah's flesh, quite as effectually as a coffin, or a tomb, or the gradual decay of some quiet and concealed grave."[20]

Tertullian describes Jonah's death in disgusting, horrific detail. He also describes the gradual dissolving of Jonah's flesh, postmortem, in the swirling stomach acids of "the bowels of the whale."

Not only was Jonah dead, but he was dead for three days. Being dead for that amount of time and then rising from the dead—*that* is the sign of Jonah. Christ Himself, in His own Resurrection, provides the sign of Jonah by being really, truly dead for three days before that Resurrection

In promising that they will see the sign of Jonah, Jesus is directly telling the crowds about His upcoming death and Resurrection. And, just as the masses in Nineveh repented after Jonah rose from the dead, so will massive conversions follow the Resurrection of Jesus.[21] Of course, we should note that Jesus also says, "Something greater than Jonah is here." Jesus is greater than Jonah. God restored life to Jonah, but Jesus is God. Jesus will resurrect *Himself*.

---

[20] Tertullian, "Even Unburied Bodies Will Be Raised Again. Whatever Befalls Them God Will Restore Them Again. Jonah's Case Quoted in Illustration of God's Power," chapter 32 of *Ante-Nicene Fathers*, vol. 3.

[21] The Ninevites were pagan Gentiles. Likewise, massive conversions of Gentiles will follow Jesus' Resurrection. It is possible that Jesus even referred to the sign of Jonah in the Court of the Gentiles, the outer court of the Temple where Gentiles were permitted to worship, which was made a "den of thieves" by the money changers.

Also, look at the word God uses when He speaks to Jonah's lifeless body, Jonah's *corpse*, which the fish vomits unceremoniously onto the seashore. God says to him, "*Arise*, go to Nineveh, that great city, and proclaim to it the message that I tell you."

Do this word choice and phrasing sound familiar? *Arise* is the Hebrew word *qum* or קוּם. Jesus uses the same word in Aramaic when He raises Jairus's daughter from the dead.[22] According to Mark 5:41, Jesus "[took] her by the hand [and] he said to her, 'Talitha cumi,' which means, 'Little girl, I say to you, arise.'"

Jesus' discussion of the sign of Jonah does not end there; look how Jesus again uses the word *arise* in Matthew 12:38-42 (emphasis added):

Then some of the scribes and Pharisees said to him, "Teacher, we wish to see a sign from you." But he answered them, "An evil and adulterous generation seeks for a sign; but no sign shall be given to it except the sign of the prophet Jonah. For as Jonah was three days and three nights in the belly of the whale, so will the Son of man be three days and three nights in the heart of the earth. The men of Nineveh will *arise* at the judgment with this generation and condemn it; for they repented at the preaching of Jonah, and behold, something greater than Jonah is here. The queen of the South will *arise* at the judgment with this generation and condemn it; for she came from the ends of the earth to hear the wisdom of Solomon, and behold, something greater than Solomon is here.

[22] Jesus uses the same command to raise from the dead the widow of Nain's son in Luke 7:14-15: "And he came and touched the bier, and the bearers stood still. And he said, 'Young man, I say to you, *arise*.' And the dead man sat up and began to speak. And he gave him to his mother."

Jesus, who is the ultimate interpreter of the Old Testament, is using the word *arise* to describe the men of Nineveh and the queen of the South (Sheba) rising from their graves. He is expanding on the theme of Jonah and Himself rising from the dead, including the men of Nineveh and the queen of the South in that understanding; like Jonah and Him, they are described as rising from the dead.

Jonah's Second Rising?

At this juncture, we might stop and ask: Who was Jonah? And where did he come from? The book of Jonah does not tell us much about his origins, and he is, in some ways, a mysterious figure. His entire predicament can even seem a bit ridiculous at first glance. Why does God call him to preach repentance to Nineveh? And why does he then respond by attempting to flee around the world, rather than accept that mission?

It all seems very mysterious—unless we have some other way of knowing who Jonah is. All we know from this book of the Bible is that he is "the son of Amittai" (Jon. 1:1). Outside of the book of Jonah and the references that Jesus makes to him, the Bible mentions Jonah only once more. 2 Kings 14:25 states (emphasis added) that the restoration of the borders of Israel by Jeroboam II against foreign invaders fulfilled the "word of the LORD the God of Israel, which he spoke by his servant Jonah the *son of Amittai, the prophet, who was from Gath-hepher.*"

This answers part of the mystery. Jonah had some notoriety as a prophet. Perhaps word of him had even spread to Nineveh.

There's more. There is an ancient tradition that Jonah is mentioned again in the Bible, though not by name. Many commentators, both Christian and Jewish, believe that Jonah is actually the son of the widow of Zarephath, who was *resuscitated* by Elijah (1 Kings 17:17–23).

Isn't that incredible? That would make Jonah the only figure in the entire Bible to have been raised from the dead *twice*.

This ancient tradition is attested to by St. Jerome[23] and Pseudo-Epiphanius,[24] as well as in the Midrash, which is the collected writings and biblical commentary of the ancient Jewish rabbis.[25] Jonah is also frequently depicted in ancient artwork as a symbol of resurrection.[26]

The Midrash provides more details that help us make sense of the mysterious figure of Jonah. In that text, after being raised from the dead by Elijah, Jonah followed in the line of the prophets of Israel, eventually succeeding Elijah and Elisha. After Elijah was assumed into Heaven on a fiery chariot, Elisha took on Elijah's mantle of prophecy and Jonah became Elisha's disciple.[27]

There's still more. The ancient Jews contributed not only to the beginning of his story but also to the end. Like Elijah, the Midrash describes Jonah as one of the people who did not die but who was instead taken up or assumed bodily into Paradise. The

---

[23] Commentaries, in Jonas, Prol., PL XXV, 118.

[24] *De Vitis Prophetarum* 16, PL XLIII, 407. In *De Vitis Prophetarum*, one finds a mention of Jonah's family: Jonah's mother is a widow, and having returned from Nineveh, he takes her with him and flees to Tyre in order to avoid being scorned as a false prophet. He dies there, but Elijah resurrects him, "because he wanted to show him that he cannot escape God."

[25] Yer. Suk. v. 1; Gen. R. xcviii.11; Yalḳ, Jonah, 550; Abravanel's commentary to Jonah; Pirḳe R. El. Xxxiii.

[26] Jonah is frequently used as a symbol of resurrection in ancient artwork. See Bezalel Narkiss, "The Sign of Jonah," *Papers Related to Objects in the Exhibition "Age of Spirituality"* 18, no. 1, Metropolitan Museum of Art (Chicago: University of Chicago Press, 1979), 63–76.

[27] 2 Kings 9; Ḳimḥhi, ad loc., and Ẓemaḥ Dawid.

Rabbis relate that Jonah, being completely righteous, would enter the Garden of Eden while still alive.[28]

Jonah ascending into Heaven like Elijah adds yet another component to the "sign of Jonah." Like Jonah, Jesus will die for three days, rise, and later ascend to Heaven.

Jonah's Near-Death Experience

Wait a second. Jonah died. Jonah went to Sheol, to the pit. God restored Jonah to life. And Jonah himself also provided us with an account of his experience. Let's return to Jonah's prayer to God as he descends to the underworld. As you read, you may begin to feel claustrophobic, for Jonah is calling to God from a place like a prison: "The waters closed in over me, the deep was round about me, weeds were wrapped about my head at the roots of the mountains. I went down to the land whose bars closed upon me for ever" (Jon. 2:5–6).

The water "closed in over" Jonah. The deep was "round about" him. Weeds encircled his head, choking him. Finally, the "bars" of the earth closed in on him "for ever."

Clearly, Jonah had an NDE. And Jonah's full prayer (Jon. 2:2–9, quoted above) is the account of that NDE. Jonah's effect on Nineveh, following his NDE, is also significant. Now let's analyze Jonah's account as an NDE.

---

[28] In Midrash Tehillim 26:7, Jonah is given a highly laudatory description as "a completely righteous man (קידצ רומג), who was purified by a fish who swallowed him and by deep waters, but did not die … ascending to Paradise alive with honor." This statement that Jonah "did not die" may have led to some confusion about Jonah not dying in the belly of the fish. The meaning of "did not die" here is not in reference to the fish but his believed assumption into heaven, i.e., the next line: "ascending to Paradise alive with honor."

Here again is Jonah's prayer to God as he descends into the depth of Sheol: "I called to the LORD, out of my distress, and he answered me; out of the belly of Sheol I cried, and thou didst hear my voice. For thou didst cast me into the deep, into the heart of the seas, and the flood was round about me; all thy waves and thy billows passed over me" (Jon. 2:2–3).

As we discussed earlier, the location of Jonah's NDE is not Heaven or Hell, but Sheol. This makes Jonah's NDE unique, as most of them describe visits to Heaven.

What Is Sheol?

We've talked about this already, but it's worth going back for a bit of a deeper understanding. *Sheol* is the Hebrew term for the underworld.[29] In the Septuagint, the Hebrew term שְׁאוֹל (she'ol) was translated as the Greek term ἅδης (hadēs), which referred to both the netherworld and to the Greek god of the netherworld.[30] Apart from Jonah's account, scriptural descriptions of Sheol are sparse, but it's generally described as "a somnolent, gloomy existence without meaningful activity or social distinction."[31]

In Christian terms, we might say that Sheol is the equivalent of Purgatory, or at least its precursor. It is a place of waiting, a place that ultimately leads to Heaven. This underlying search for hope in the midst of darkness is communicated when Jonah says, "I am cast out from thy presence; how shall I again look upon thy holy temple?" (Jon. 2:4).

---

[29] Philip S. Johnston, *Shades of Sheol: Death and Afterlife in the Old Testament* (Downers Grove, IL: InterVarsity Press, 2002), 74–75.

[30] Martin A. Shields, "Death," in *The Lexham Bible Dictionary*, ed. John D. Barry et al. (Bellingham, WA: Lexham Press, 2016).

[31] Shields, "Death."

Jonah describes being exiled, "cast out," from God's presence. He is beyond the sight of God. Nevertheless, he remains faithful to God. He does not give in to despair. Jonah keeps his eyes fixed on Heaven, yearning for God's holy temple there.

This accurately describes the disposition of the souls in Purgatory, as well as the Sheol of Jonah. St. Margaret Mary was often besought by souls from Purgatory seeking relief from their torments. St. Margaret Mary said of these suffering souls: "If only you knew with what great longing these holy souls yearn for relief from their suffering. Ingratitude has never entered Heaven."[32]

St. Faustina Kowalska provided a similar observation of the souls in Purgatory after something she went through that was similar to an NDE. She was taken to "a misty place full of fire" by her guardian angel:

> I saw my guardian angel, who ordered me to follow him. In a moment I was in a misty place full of fire in which there was a great crowd of suffering souls. They were praying fervently, but to no avail, for themselves; only we can come to their aid. The flames, which were burning them, did not touch me at all. My guardian angel did not leave me for an instant. I asked these souls what their greatest suffering was. They answered me in one voice that their greatest torment was longing for God.[33]

---

[32] St. Margaret Mary in her letter to Mother de Saumaise, at Dijon, May 2, 1683, *Letters of St. Margaret Mary Alacoque*, 32, Saints' Works, https://www.saintsworks.net/books/St.%20Margaret%20Mary%20Alacoque%20-%20Letters.pdf.

[33] *Diary of Saint Maria Faustina Kowalska: Divine Mercy in My Soul* (Stockbridge, MA: Marian Press, 2003), no. 20.

It bears repeating that St. Faustina reveals here that the greatest torment of the souls in Purgatory is not burning in the flames, but their "longing for God."

A Life Forever Changed

One of the consistent characteristics of NDEs is the positive change they cause in their survivors' lives. As I noted in the introduction, this has been consistently documented in medical studies.

After Jonah's descent into the prison of the depths, he suddenly demonstrates the gratitude that St. Margaret Mary described above, as well as the longing and yearning for the sanctuary of God's holy temple:

> Yet thou didst bring up my life from the Pit, O LORD my God. When my soul fainted within me, I remembered the LORD; and my prayer came to thee, into thy holy temple. Those who pay regard to vain idols forsake their true loyalty. But I with the voice of thanksgiving will sacrifice to thee; what I have vowed I will pay. Deliverance belongs to the LORD! (Jon. 2:6–9)

Jonah ends his prayer in the "voice of thanksgiving." He will repay God's faithfulness to him with his own faithfulness to God.

2

DID ST. PAUL HAVE A NEAR-DEATH EXPERIENCE?

In the Acts of the Apostles, we see the stoning of St. Stephen, the man who is widely held to be the first Christian martyr. Although we can't rightly say that he had a *near*-death experience as he did die and was not restored to life, we do read an account of his last moments, in which he experienced a theophany. That is, he saw and spoke of God:

> But [St. Stephen], full of the Holy Spirit, gazed into heaven and saw the glory of God, and Jesus standing at the right hand of God; and he said, "Behold, I see the heavens opened, and the Son of man standing at the right hand of God." But they cried out with a loud voice and stopped their ears and rushed together upon him. (Acts 7:55–57)

Now, do you remember who assisted in the stoning of St. Stephen? It was Saul, the future St. Paul. Wouldn't it be interesting if St. Paul, who was so intimately involved in bringing St. Stephen to his death, also had such a moment of experiencing the Divine while still on earth? And what if St. Paul had an NDE, that, like St. Stephen's encounter, occurred as a result of a stoning?

Surviving Stoning?

First off, before his final martyrdom, was St. Paul ever near death? I would argue that our Bibles would burst if they contained the full details of every time St. Paul was killed, almost killed, going to be killed, or a crowd attempted to kill him.

Because St. Paul faced death on so many occasions, how are we to know which brush with death was *the one?*

St. Luke provides us with a clue in this mysterious passage from the book of Acts: "But Jews came there from Antioch and Iconium; and having persuaded the people, they stoned Paul and dragged him out of the city, supposing that he was dead. But when the disciples gathered about him, he rose up and entered the city; and on the next day he went on with Barnabas to Derbe" (14:19–20).

St. Paul survived stoning. Let's sit with this point for a moment. This is an incredible statement.

The act of stoning a person is so monstrously violent that people rarely survive it. In fact, St. Paul is the *only* person in the Bible to have survived being stoned.

Let's say that again: St. Paul is the *only* person in the Bible who survived stoning.

It doesn't take many large stones thrown or brought down on a person's head to seriously injure him. The reason people keep throwing stones is not to kill the person they're stoning. The reason is to kill the person *quickly*, to end his hideous suffering. Under ordinary circumstances, the victim of a stoning is a dead man from the beginning.

Also note that St. Paul isn't running out of Lystra in a hail of stones: "They stoned Paul and dragged him out of the city, supposing that he was dead." First, they stoned him. Then they dragged his lifeless body out of the city. This tells us that St. Paul was executed by stoning *inside* the city. There is some formality to this process.

What Happens during an Execution by Stoning?

This mental image of a stoning, conjuring up pictures of a mob throwing baseball- or even softball-size stones, requires some adjustment. First, as I just noted, St. Paul's stoning occurred *inside* the city's walls, where law abides—not beyond the city walls, where the mob rules.

Now, before we get into the details of what happens in a stoning, I do want to warn you that the discussion can get pretty gruesome. If you want to skip this section, just know that there was an entire process set out in the Mishna—a written collection of Jewish custom and law, gathered from previous centuries of oral tradition, dating back hundreds of years before the birth of Christ—to ensure that death would result from a stoning.

Since I am an attorney by trade, reading these civil and criminal laws of first- and second-century A.D. Israel is fascinating to me. From a lawyer's perspective, the Jewish legal system was very sophisticated, even advanced, and shows a surprising degree of concern for the dignity of the human person—even though it did allow for execution by stoning.

It should first be noted that stoning was a judicial method of execution, a court proceeding. It was not a mob activity.

The fourth Order of the Mishna, the Nezikin,[34] describes the Jewish criminal and civil law and the Jewish court system of the first and second centuries A.D. Tractate Sanhedrin deals with the death penalty and other criminal matters, including the specific procedure required for a stoning. According to this tractate, stones were not thrown at the condemned man, at least not at the beginning of the process. The condemned man was *pushed* to his death,

---

[34] Hebrew: נזיקין, Nezikin, "Damages"; or סדר נזיקין, Seder Nezikin "The Order of Damages."

from a "platform twice the height of an ordinary person." Falling from this height was intended to kill a man humanely—this should, of course, sound like a very strange statement. The platform is also constructed at this specific height to avoid disfigurement. The condemned man "is made to stand at the edge of the platform, and then one of the witnesses who testified against him pushes him down by the hips." This method ensured that the condemned man fell "face up onto the ground," instead of headfirst. Again, this is an attempt to avoid disfigurement or an overly gruesome and prolonged death.[35]

If the condemned man survived the fall, only then were stones used in what we likely first think of as a stoning. The Mishna dictates that the second witness against the condemned person would be the one to "cast the first stone." In Scripture, we see a variation on this phrase in John 8:7, when Jesus invites anyone without sin to be "first to throw a stone" at the woman caught in adultery.[36]

There is no random grabbing of stones. The second witness "takes the stone that has been prepared for this task" and casts it onto the condemned man's chest.

And if the one being stoned should still be alive after all that? It is only then, the Mishna directs, that "his stoning is completed by all of the Jewish people, i.e., by all the people who assembled for the execution." This fulfills what is prescribed in Deuteronomy: "The hand of the witnesses shall be first against him to put him to death, and afterward the hand of all the people" (Deut. 17:7).

---

[35] Mishna Tractate Sanhedrin 45a, v. 10.

[36] There is also a tradition that the duly appointed presiding official or judge casts the first stone. This may give some additional insight into Jesus' words about letting the one who is free of sin cast the first stone. The stoning of the woman caught in adultery also may have been improper because it was unsanctioned by a court process.

This gives us some insight into the question: Did St. Paul survive stoning? The methodical approach to stoning carried out by the Jewish court system makes this outcome unlikely. It is far more likely that St. Paul did *not* survive this execution.

Look also to the response of the disciples, which gives us an important insight. Read this next verse carefully: "But when the disciples gathered about him, he rose up" (Acts 14:20). Why are the disciples gathering around St. Paul? Is it to gawk at his mangled body?

When I was a missionary in Nairobi, I once came upon the bodies of men who were stoned to death. It was a grisly sight, one I will always remember. It was also a pitiable sight. The poor men! These were not innocent men, mind you. But in witnessing the effects of such a death—their poor, crumpled forms—pity is a natural reaction.

What did I do? I immediately stopped and began praying for them. It felt like the most natural thing to do. This also seems like the most natural reaction for the disciples upon seeing the ruined body of their friend Paul. On that day in Nairobi, I saw strangers, even criminals—but the disciples who gathered around St. Paul saw their brother.

What might they have been praying for as they approached him? Only two things could make sense in that context. Either they were praying for the repose of St. Paul's soul or they were praying for his healing. And, at this point, healing would mean rising from the dead.

What happens next is critical to our understanding of this entire episode. Prayer is the cause—but what is the effect?

St. Paul "rose up." Whatever the disciples were doing when they gathered around his body, the effect was that St. Paul "rose up."

Does the use of this phrase signify rising from the dead?

Interestingly, these two phrases "gathered about him" and "rose up" occur together in only one other location in the New Testament: during the account of Jesus' healing Jairus's daughter in Mark 5. Yes, *that* Jairus—the one whose daughter was *raised from the dead* by Jesus.

Remember that in Mark 5:41, Jesus takes the girl by the hand and says to her, "*Talitha cumi*," which means, "Little girl, I say to you, *arise*." "Arise," or *cumi*, is the word that the Word of God Himself uses to restore life to the twelve-year-old girl.[37]

What Happened to St. Paul When He Died?

If indeed St. Paul was stoned to death, died, and was raised, what happened in the intervening time? Did St. Paul have an NDE? And if so, what did he see?

The above passage from the Acts of the Apostles provides little information. As we just saw, if we read it too fast, we can easily gloss over the likelihood that St. Paul died and was restored to life. As we are not given a lot of information in this passage about what he might have seen during his NDE, let us turn to a different book in the Bible.

St. Paul relates the following experience, which he almost seems bashful about, in 2 Corinthians 12:2–4:

[37] There is another interesting connection between the account of St. Paul's resurrection and Mark 5 that involves the chronological span of twelve years. In Mark 5, Jesus heals two people linked by a span of twelve years, which represents the duration of the woman's illness (Mark 5:25) and the age of the young girl (Mark 5:42). Like Jairus's daughter, St. Paul is also something of a twelve-year-old when he is stoned to death. Depending on how you count the years, St. Paul's conversion to Christianity—his rebirth as a Christian—on the road to Damascus occurred twelve years prior to his stoning at Lystra.

I know a man in Christ who fourteen years ago was caught up to the third heaven—whether in the body or out of the body I do not know, God knows. And I know that this man was caught up into Paradise—whether in the body or out of the body I do not know, God knows—and he heard things that cannot be told, which man may not utter.

That's straightforward, right? A man "caught up to the third heaven," "out of the body," and "heard things that cannot be told." That's the basic formula for an NDE, right in the middle of 2 Corinthians.

Let's unpack these verses a bit.

Whom did this happen to? St. Paul says, "I know a man in Christ" who had this experience. It is generally accepted that St. Paul is referring to himself, as the use of "I know a man" was a form of personal modesty in ancient times. And this supposition is confirmed just a few verses later when he says (emphasis added), "And to keep *me* from being too elated by the abundance of revelations, a thorn was given me in the flesh" (2 Cor. 12:7). Not only does this confirm that St. Paul is telling us about his own experience, but it also tells us that he was truly overwhelmed by the experience of Paradise and the Third Heaven.

What Is the Third Heaven?

Does this terminology mean that there are three Heavens? No.

The Hebrew word for *heaven*, *shamayim*, is plural: *heavens*, not *heaven*. This would suggest at least two heavens, or even a multiplicity of heavens. Some ancient sources speak of up to *ten* heavens. There is even the expression *seventh heaven*, meaning a "state of extreme joy."[38]

---

[38] Merriam-Webster.

What does all this mean? Are there multiple spiritual realms?

In Hebrew, the word for *heaven* is also the word for *sky* or *lofty*. It may be that St. Paul's count includes the physical heavens — that is, the sky and clouds sprinkled with rainbows and birds that we can see. This would be the First Heaven. What, then, is the Second Heaven? This would be the "celestial" heaven of stars and other planets. And this means that the Third Heaven would be the "empyrean" Heaven, the dwelling place of God.

With this understanding, then, we can make the argument that when St. Paul speaks of being "caught up to the third heaven," he is not describing multiple spiritual realms. He means he entered the presence of God.

St. Paul confirms this in 2 Corinthians 12:4, when he reiterates his experience. This time, he says he was "caught up into Paradise." St. Paul describes "third heaven" and "Paradise" as synonymous.

St. Paul's Encounter with the Third Heaven: A Near-Death Experience?

The phrasing of these verses in 2 Corinthians indicates a sort of sequential passage through the Heavens: St. Paul passes from earth to First Heaven to Second Heaven to Third Heaven. This tracks with the "tunnel experience" of passing spatially from this place to the next. Even the phrase "caught up" could indicate the rapid flight of the soul "out of the body."

If not fully an NDE, St. Paul's experience does seem to have at least been an OBE. How do we know this? Because St. Paul said it himself in 2 Corinthians 12:3. He says (emphasis added), "Whether in the body or *out of the body* I do not know, God knows."

So we have this scriptural confirmation that he did have an OBE or something near to it, but can we say that St. Paul's OBE was also an NDE?

As described above, St. Paul seemed to be always near death. Look at his account of his beatings and dangers described in 2 Corinthians 11:23–29 (emphases added):

… with far greater labors, far more imprisonments, with countless beatings, and *often near death.* Five times I have received at the hands of the Jews the forty lashes less one. Three times I have been beaten with rods; *once I was stoned.* Three times I have been shipwrecked; a night and a day I have been adrift at sea; on frequent journeys, in danger from rivers, danger from robbers, danger from my own people, danger from Gentiles, danger in the city, danger in the wilderness, danger at sea, danger from false brethren; in toil and hardship, through many a sleepless night, in hunger and thirst, often without food, in cold and exposure. And, apart from other things, there is the daily pressure upon me of my anxiety for all the churches. Who is weak, and I am not weak? Who is made to fall, and I am not indignant?

Did you catch that? St. Paul actually uses the phrase "near death" (emphasized above) to describe his many violent experiences, most of which happened multiple times. If that's not enough, these two passages from St. Paul that we've talked about, in which he describes both being "near death" and "out of body," occur *right* next to another: They are both in 2 Corinthians, the first at the end of chapter 11 and the second at the beginning of chapter 12. With all of this in mind, I propose that St. Paul had both an NDE and an OBE.

I also want to take a moment to note that the term *near-death experience* was derived from a French phrase, *expérience de mort imminente,* or *experience of imminent death.* Although this phrase, in its contemporary usage, was first coined by French psychologist and epistemologist Victor Egger in the 1890s, in reference to the experiences of hikers who fell to their near deaths in the French Alps, we must not give Egger too much credit. We have seen clearly at this point that both of these phrases—NDE and OBE—originated in the Bible.

3

ST. JOHN AND THE BOOK OF REVELATION

While not an NDE, we can consider the entire book of Revelation as one long OBE. St. John's apocalyptic vision is, quite simply, the most detailed account of Heaven in existence. It is also the one by which all others should be judged, as it forms part of the canon of Scripture.

The Actual Title of the Book of Revelation

You have likely heard some people use a different name for the book of Revelation; sometimes it is referred to as the *Apocalypse* according to St. John, a name that is derived from the first words of the first verse. Although "revelation" is a legitimate translation of the Greek word *apokalypsis* (apocalypse), some of the meaning of the original is lost in this common translation.

An *apocalypse* is an *unveiling*. The veil that separates this world from Heaven was pulled away for St. John, that he might see the true reality. After the Fall, our eyes were opened to our nakedness (Gen. 3:7), but they were closed to heavenly realities—including the sight of God and the war of angels and demons that surrounds us. In the book of Revelation, that veil is removed from God's plan for the future. The curtain that hides Christ's

45

glory, kingship, and control over history is drawn back from the naked eye.[39]

In this sense, all NDEs and OBEs are a kind of apocalypse or unveiling. God grants a kind of sight akin to that which He first granted to humanity—the kind of vision that was lost to all mankind when our first parents committed Original Sin.

We usually think of the word *apocalypse* in terms of the final Apocalypse. We think of Armageddon and the final battle and victory of Heaven over Hell. Of course, from God's perspective, this has happened, is happening, and will happen—in the eternal now.

The more general sense of this *apocalypse*, the unveiling of our eyes, is imminently relevant to our present inquiry. St. John's experience on the island of Patmos should inform our study of OBEs and perhaps of NDEs. At the same time, our outside study of other similar experiences may also inform our understanding of the book of Revelation. We might see this book with new insights, for, as we read in Revelation 21:5: "Behold, I make all things new."

Was St. John Near Death?

There is reason to believe that St. John was near death when he received his vision of Heaven and the Apocalypse.

Our first evidence for this comes from the book of Revelation itself. St. John begins describing his vision at 1:9: "I, John, your brother, who share with you in Jesus the tribulation and the kingdom and the patient endurance, was on the island of Patmos on account of the word of God and the testimony of Jesus."

St. John states that he is sharing in the "tribulation" with "patient endurance." The Greek word that is translated here as "tribulation" is *thlipsis*, which means "affliction" or "distress." This

---

[39] See *Catechism of the Catholic Church* (CCC), paragraph 50.

same word is found in Matthew 24:9 (emphasis added): "Then they will deliver you up to *tribulation*, and put you to death." With this linguistic connection, I posit that St. John's words suggest he is patiently enduring a time of affliction and close brushes with death.

Additionally, John says in Revelation 1:17 that, when he saw the Lord, he "fell at his feet as though dead."

St. John's location—the island of Patmos—is revelatory as well. He experienced his vision while he was exiled to this small island. According to the tradition preserved by Irenaeus, Eusebius, Jerome, and others, St. John was exiled to Patmos in the fourteenth year of the reign of the Roman emperor Domitian, and he was subsequently released to Ephesus under Nerva, circa A.D. 96.[40]

Not much is known about the first-century history of Patmos. It is a Greek island in the Aegean Sea near the western coast of Turkey. The place on the island where St. John received his visions, the Cave of the Apocalypse, is still an important pilgrimage and tourist destination.[41]

For the Romans, Patmos was a penal colony. Criminals were exiled to this barren rock in the middle of the sea, not unlike the island of Alcatraz. People who were sent there often starved to death, as food was scarce and needed to be supplied directly by the Romans. With this history in mind, on top of the scriptural evidence provided above, it is probable that St. John was near death—from starvation—at the time of his visions. But there is more too. Starvation may have been the least of St. John's worries.

On the order of Emperor Domitian, St. John was thrown into a cauldron of boiling oil, but he was miraculously preserved from

---

[40] John D. Barry et al., eds., "Patmos," *Lexham Bible Dictionary*.

[41] The Cave of the Apocalypse is part of the complex of the Monastery of St. John the Theologian.

injury.[42] It was after this miraculous survival that he was exiled to Patmos.

A noncanonical fifth-century work *Acts of John by Prochorus* also claims to be a chronicle of St. John's experiences on Patmos.[43] According to the *Acts of John by Prochorus*, St. John experienced not just prolonged starvation but also multiple shipwrecks and earthquakes during his journey into exile and while on the island of Patmos.[44] There is also an account of St. John's being killed by an angry mob and then returning to life. *Yes!* St. John may have had an NDE much like that of St. Paul—it is possible that both were killed by angry mobs *and* raised from the dead.

Given these accounts, St. John could likely have received his apocalyptic visions while near death. We cannot know this for certain, however, and tradition holds otherwise—and I defer to tradition. Nevertheless, elements of St. John's OBE may enlighten us concerning elements of NDEs.

These visions may also have occurred while St. John was celebrating Mass. St. John states that his inaugural vision occurred on "the Lord's day," which is Sunday, the first day of the week,

---

[42] John Gilmary Shea, *Pictorial Lives of the Saints* (New York: Benziger Brothers, 1887), 508.

[43] The *Acts of John by Prochorus* claims to narrate the miraculous deeds of the apostle John in Asia Minor and on Patmos from the perspective of a person named Prochorus, whom the text pseudonymously claims as its narrator. Prochorus is one of the deacons mentioned in Acts 6:5. However, the text was actually written around the fifth century A.D. (de Santos Otero, "Later Acts," 430–431). Jason S. Sturdevant, "Acts of John by Prochorus," ed. John D. Barry et al., *Lexham Bible Dictionary.*

[44] Ian Boxall, "Patmos as Narrative World: The *Acts of John by Prochorus*," in *Patmos in the Reception History of the Apocalypse* (Oxford, UK: Oxford University Press, 2013), 106–114.

when Christians gather for the liturgy that commemorates the Resurrection of Jesus (Acts 20:7; Luke 24:1–7; CCC 1166–1167). Indeed, one might even argue that it is impossible to make sense of John's visions outside of the Holy Mass, for the Divine Liturgy is the central image and paradigm of the book of Revelation.

Did St. John Have a Tunnel Experience?

St. John's description of Heaven is remarkable for its level of detail. St. John surpasses all the prophets—Isaiah, Ezekiel, and even Daniel—in the breadth and scope of his vision. He received a firsthand glimpse into the heavenly courts unlike any of his predecessors. He begins in Revelation 1:10: "I was in the Spirit on the Lord's day."

What does it mean that he was "in the Spirit"? One might argue that he is saying that he was not in his own body, that he had been taken up and out into another realm, similar to the descriptions we see from people who have had NDEs in which they've found themselves in something like a tunnel. This language of being "in the Spirit" is also similar to St. Paul's experience of being *caught up to the third heaven*" (2 Cor. 12:2–4).

John is seized by the Spirit while engaged in prayer and worship (Rev. 1:10).[45] He is then transported to several locations. He is carried off into Heaven (Rev. 4:2), into the wilderness (Rev. 17:3), and then to the summit of a high mountain (Rev. 21:10). Ezekiel was similarly transported by the Spirit (Ezek. 2:2; 3:14; 11:1; 40:2). These transportations bear the hallmarks of an intellectual vision or locution.

---

[45] See the explanatory footnote in Curtis Mitch and Scott Hahn, eds., *The Ignatius Catholic Study Bible: The New Testament* (San Francisco: Ignatius Press, 2010), 494.

St. John's Description of the "Being of Light"

It would take an entire book—possibly an entire library of books—to examine thoroughly St. John's rich descriptions of Heaven. Knowing that our examination of it will barely scratch the surface, we will nonetheless do our best to analyze some key moments from John's visions.

St. John borrows and builds on the images from the sweeping visions of the prophets Ezekiel and Daniel. We discussed Daniel's visions of God at the beginning of this chapter; what he saw was similar to the "being of light" that is so often described in NDEs. In John's account, this being had hair that was exceedingly white, like that of Daniel's "one that was ancient of days" (Dan. 7:9). The Lord's voice is like the rumbling of God's glory when it draws near, as described by Ezekiel (Ezek. 43:2).

The Lord's appearance also resembles "one like a son of man" and is of surpassing brightness (Dan. 7:13). His eyes were like torches, "like a flame of fire" (Rev 1:14). The Lord's feet, too, gleam like bronze fired in a furnace (Dan. 10:6).

John, like the prophets before him, also falls prostrate before the exalted Lord, as though dead (Rev. 1:17; Ezek. 1:28; 44:4; Dan. 10:9)—another suggestion that this might have been an actual NDE, not just an OBE!

St. John Describes the Heavenly City

Many NDEs include descriptions of a vast city of light and a vast blinding land of light. In Revelation 21:9–14, St. John describes the heavenly city of Jerusalem as somewhat akin to all of that, depicting it in exquisite detail (emphasis added):

Then came one of the seven angels who had the seven bowls full of the seven last plagues, and spoke to me, saying,

"Come, I will show you the Bride, the wife of the Lamb." *And in the Spirit* he carried me away to a great, high mountain, and showed me the holy city Jerusalem coming down out of heaven from God, having the glory of God, its radiance like a most rare jewel, like a jasper, clear as crystal. It had a great, high wall, with twelve gates, and at the gates twelve angels, and on the gates the names of the twelve tribes of the sons of Israel were inscribed; on the east three gates, on the north three gates, on the south three gates, and on the west three gates. And the wall of the city had twelve foundations, and on them the twelve names of the twelve apostles of the Lamb.

Further, St. John reminds us that there will be no more tears, death, crying, or pain in Heaven. In Revelation 21:22–27, he describes the Temple of the New Jerusalem, which is Jesus:

And I saw no temple in the city, for its temple is the Lord God the Almighty and the Lamb. And the city has no need of sun or moon to shine upon it, for the glory of God is its light, and its lamp is the Lamb. By its light shall the nations walk; and the kings of the earth shall bring their glory into it, and its gates shall never be shut by day—and there shall be no night there; they shall bring into it the glory and the honor of the nations. But nothing unclean shall enter it, nor anyone who practices abomination or falsehood, but only those who are written in the Lamb's book of life.

While St. John does narrate the judgment of the nations, his vision is ultimately one of surpassing hope for mankind and its ultimate destiny in union with God.

St. John's Vision of the Blessed Mother as Queen of Heaven

Many NDEs, such as that of Fr. Steven Scheier, also describe a beautiful lady who reigns as queen in Heaven. Just so, in Revelation 12:1–5, St. John provides the iconic image of the Virgin Mary as the Queen of Heaven:

> And a great portent appeared in heaven, a woman clothed with the sun, with the moon under her feet, and on her head a crown of twelve stars; she was with child and she cried out in her pangs of birth, in anguish for delivery. And another portent appeared in heaven; behold, a great red dragon, with seven heads and ten horns, and seven diadems upon his heads. His tail swept down a third of the stars of heaven, and cast them to the earth. And the dragon stood before the woman who was about to bear a child, that he might devour her child when she brought it forth; she brought forth a male child, one who is to rule all the nations with a rod of iron, but her child was caught up to God and to his throne.

St. John sees so much of salvation history fulfilled and occurring in this one vision. Namely, Jesus is being born of the Blessed Mother, whom He crowns *following* His own death and Resurrection. On top of this, John sees the fall of the angels as the dragon's tail sweeps "down a third of the stars of heaven."

As we wrap up our discussion of St. John's visions, there is one key thing to note that separates what he saw from what other people who have had OBEs and NDEs have seen. Most people's experiences either allow them to observe something happening to themselves or give them a glimpse of the afterlife in some form. But John's visions are not just observations; they are prophecies. Whatever his experiences were, they provide us with something the likes of which almost no other OBE or NDE touches.

Part II

NEAR-DEATH EXPERIENCES OF THE SAINTS

Some saints have such extensive accounts of NDEs that we can—and will!—spend entire chapters of this book just talking about what they saw and learned. While there are many more than the four whom we'll primarily focus on in the following chapters—indeed, every time I turn around, I seem to find more examples of NDEs (and OBEs) in the lives of saints whom I thought I already knew well—we have to draw the line somewhere. To that end, I've decided to share with you just some of the more striking experiences I've come across in my study of the lives of the saints, things that happened to them directly or that they witnessed in the lives of others. We will particularly focus on St. Teresa of Ávila, St. Thérèse of Lisieux, Pope St. Gregory the Great, and Padre Pio.

4

ST. TERESA OF ÁVILA

Did you know that St. Teresa of Ávila, when she was in her early twenties, was dead for four days before being brought back to life?[46] Her sister Carmelites had already covered her eyes in wax, something that was done in that day and age in preparation for burial. They had even had a funeral Mass already celebrated for her. Her tomb was prepared and waiting.

St. Teresa later wrote the tale of this "paroxysm," or what we now know as her own NDE, in her autobiography and briefly in her masterpiece, *The Interior Castle*. The quotations in her own words, recounted in the pages below, are from the fifth chapter of her autobiography.

St. Teresa's Four Days of Death

In 1537, St. Teresa was twenty-two years old. Despite having wanted to become a nun for some time, she had only recently entered the Carmelite monastery, as her father, a widower, had previously forbidden it. He wanted his daughter to stay home and look after him and his estate. St. Teresa remained obedient to her father until she reached adulthood. Leaving her father, however, disturbed her greatly, both spiritually and physically.

[46] August 15–19, 1539.

Her sickness eventually grew very serious, as she describes in her autobiography: "My fainting fits began to increase in number, and I suffered so much from heart trouble that everyone who saw me was alarmed.... My condition became so serious—for I hardly ever seemed to be fully conscious, and sometimes I lost consciousness altogether—that my father made great efforts to find me a cure."[47]

In fact, her health problems became so bad that she had to leave the convent, as the other Carmelite nuns were not equipped to care for her. When she returned home, her father tried various remedies to help her recover, but nothing worked.

On August 15, 1537, the feast of the Assumption of the Blessed Virgin Mary, St. Teresa finally lost consciousness. To nearly all observers, she appeared to have died. As noted earlier, they even prepared her grave and her body for burial:

> That night I had a seizure, which left me unconscious for nearly four days. During that time they gave me the Sacrament of Unction, and from hour to hour, from moment to moment, thought I was dying.... For a day and a half there was an open grave in my convent, where they were awaiting my body, and in one of the monasteries of our Order, some way from here, they had performed the rites for the dead.[48]

But St. Teresa's father, Don Alonso, refused to believe his daughter was dead. As a result, he did not provide consent for her burial. Thank God for this—a father's intuition![49]

---

[47] *The Life of St. Teresa of Jesus, of the Order of Our Lady of Carmel* (London: Thomas Baker, 1904), 44.

[48] *Life of St. Teresa*, 50.

[49] Perhaps it was a bit more than intuition, as, according to some sources, St. Teresa's father knew to check for her pulse, and he could feel it, however faintly.

Nevertheless, on the fourth day after her supposed death, her fellow nuns of the Incarnation Carmelite Monastery came to fetch her dead body for burial within the precincts of Carmel.

Don Alonso, however, still refused to allow his daughter to be taken away. He kept on repeating, "The time is not come for my daughter to be put under the ground."[50] The nuns and the doctors all believed that Don Alonso had gone crazy with grief. Yet he claimed to be able to hear the soft beat of Teresa's pulse. His fingers never left his daughter's wrist.

The nuns also never left Teresa's bedside. They kept praying, both on account of the young woman's death and for what they perceived to be the tragedy of her demented father.

Then, suddenly, Teresa's eyelids began to flicker. She raised her eyelids painfully, as they were weighted down by the cold wax of the funeral tapers.

Teresa found herself surrounded by the various tokens of death, as well as the *capilla ardiente*, the "burning chapel" of candles all around her. She saw she was also surrounded by her sisters, the nuns who had been waiting to carry away her corpse. Her fingers, groping and curious, fingered the shroud that encased her body. Maybe later she would reflect on Jesus Himself awakening from the sleep of death to find Himself wrapped in the burial shroud.

After four days of apparent death, St. Teresa was conscious again. Immediately, though her voice was very faint, she began asking for the sacraments. Then, a description of her experience began to pour from her.

St. Teresa's sixteenth-century biographer, Francisco de Ribera, records that, upon regaining consciousness, St. Teresa began asking,

---

[50] Marcelle Auclair, *Teresa of Avila* (New York: Pantheon, 1953), 61.

"Why did you call me back?"[51] Her later biographers opined that her initial flood of questions and statements indicated that she had not yet completely returned to earth. Teresa declared that she still had much to do in this world. Heaven had been clear on this point. But her travels had not ended in Heaven; she had seen Hell, too, and Purgatory.

When she spoke of her future work, she mentioned saving her friend and fellow nun Juana Suárez and also saving her father. (The latter she likely saved simply by returning to life.) As she tried to tell what she had seen and what she must do, her pillow was soon wet with tears. In the midst of her confused sentences, interrupted by her own sobs, as well as those of her father and sisters, they made out the words: "convents ... foundations ... to save souls."[52]

And she would indeed go on to establish many monasteries. Heaven had shown these to her.

St. Teresa's modern biographers claim that, at this point, the return of her sufferings, now more acute than ever, brought her out of her reflective trance. Her biographer Ribera likewise records that St. Teresa clammed up at this point, but for a different reason. According to Ribera, witnesses believed that Teresa silenced herself because her amazing account was bringing shame to her father, "a serious man."[53] And so she ended her account by mildly chiding her Carmelite sisters, whom she realized had attempted to bury her alive: "Don't think me dead until you see my body covered with cloth of gold."[54]

---

[51] Francisco de Ribera, *Vida de Santa Teresa de Jesús* (1590; Barcelona: Gili, 1908), 111.

[52] Auclair, *Teresa of Avila*, 61.

[53] Ribera, *Vida de Santa Teresa de Jesús*, 111.

[54] Auclair, *Teresa of Avila*, 61.

Ribera also interviewed St. Teresa's sister, Doña Juana de Ahumada, and St. Teresa's confessor, Fray Domingo Bañez,[55] professor of theology at Salamanca, regarding her later accounts of those four days. Bañez confirmed that St. Teresa had told him, in his capacity as her spiritual director, that, during these four days, she was "as if dead" and that "the Lord showed her Hell." But she did not just see Hell, as we have already mentioned; Ahumada recounted that St. Teresa "did not want to return here" because of the intense joy and beatitude that she experienced in Heaven.[56]

Now that Heaven had returned his daughter to him, Don Alonso wanted to embrace her, but she cried out with pain when he tried. The slightest touch caused her such agony "that only Our Lord can know how unbearable these sufferings were."[57]

When the bed had to be made and remade, she felt as if she were being torn to pieces. She was delirious with pain. She was also unable to lie down at full length. She was forced to stay curled up in a ball. Her muscles had utterly contracted, pulling her knees up to her chin. Unable to move "either arm, foot, hand or head,"[58] she was almost entirely paralyzed. She could move only one finger of her right hand.[59] She would remain in this pitiable state for nearly nine months. Her soul had returned to her body, but her body still behaved like a corpse, as if ready for the tomb that had been prepared for it. The day she was, at long last, freed of this

---

[55] This interview occurred in 1587 at one of the celebrations of the Discalced Carmelite Fathers, to which order he belonged.

[56] Ribera, *Vida de Santa Teresa de Jesús*.

[57] Ribera, *Vida de Santa Teresa de Jesús*.

[58] Ribera, *Vida de Santa Teresa de Jesús*.

[59] Carol Slade, *St. Teresa of Avila: Author of a Heroic Life* (Berkeley: University of California Press, 1995), 82.

intense infliction was no divine accident: She finally exited her tomb on Easter Sunday.[60]

Her patient endurance throughout her trial had amazed the entire convent of her fellow sisters, who prayed for her throughout her affliction. Even when she had complained, she still managed to find ways to express her love: "Lord, I did not want as much as this!"[61] She told them she would not exchange her sufferings for any treasure on earth.

To finally overcome her paralysis, St. Teresa appealed to St. Joseph. She would later say of him: "This glorious saint helps us in every need; Our Lord shows us that he obeys St. Joseph in heaven, just as on earth He was under him and called him Father."[62] St. Joseph prevailed on her behalf, and she never forgot him. She spread devotion to Jesus' foster-father far and wide, even effecting such devotion in a particular contemporary of hers whom we now know as St. John of the Cross. In fact, much of today's devotion to St. Joseph can be traced back to this moment when St. Teresa was healed through his intercession.

St. Teresa's Vision of Hell

St. Teresa shared the details and expounded on her encounter with Heaven and Hell throughout her life. Her autobiography describes her frightening vision of Hell and how it haunted her for the rest of her life. Writing about the vision conjured something like a post-traumatic stress disorder flashback, as she would experience the same bone-chilling feelings running through her body that she had felt when it had first been shown to her:

---

[60] The miraculous healing of St. Thérèse of Lisieux followed a similar timeline.

[61] Auclair, *Teresa of Avila*, 62.

[62] Auclair, *Teresa of Avila*, 63.

I found myself, as I thought, plunged right into Hell. I realized that it was the Lord's will that I should see the place which the devils had prepared for me there and which I had merited for my sins. This happened in the briefest space of time, but, even if I were to live for many years, I believe it would be impossible for me to forget it.[63]

This durability of Teresa's memories is a common characteristic of NDEs. Indeed, such memories are so vivid that survivors of NDEs decline to use the term *memories*. Survivors, instead, describe experiencing a flashback or reliving the experience.

St. Teresa next describes the entrance to Hell. Despite its being an entrance to Hell instead of Heaven, the "very long, narrow passage" that she mentions bears an uncanny resemblance to the tunnel experience and the light at the end of the tunnel that other survivors of NDEs have recounted:

The entrance, I thought, resembled a very long, narrow passage, like a furnace, very low, dark and closely confined; the ground seemed to be full of water which looked like filthy, evil-smelling mud, and in it were many wicked-looking reptiles. At the end there was a hollow place scooped out of a wall, like a cupboard, and it was here that I found myself in close confinement.[64]

Merely imagining an eternity of not only confinement but also extremely tight confinement is terrible enough. But that was just the beginning.

St. Teresa then describes how the feeling of the "fire within [her] soul" far exceeded her physical pains.

---

[63] *Life of St. Teresa*, chap. 32, par. 10.
[64] *Life of St. Teresa*, chap. 32, par. 2.

But the sight of all this was pleasant by comparison with what I felt there. . . . My feelings, I think, could not possibly be exaggerated, nor can anyone understand them. I felt a fire within my soul the nature of which I am utterly incapable of describing. . . . I had been put in this place which looked like a hole in the wall, and those very walls, so terrible to the sight, bore down upon me and completely stifled me. There was no light and everything was in the blackest darkness.[65]

Amazingly, Teresa describes this experience of Hell's tortures as God's "favor" to her, as a blessing. She understood why God had allowed her to see Hell's torments:

This vision was one of the most signal favors which the Lord has bestowed upon me: it has been of the greatest benefit to me, both in taking from me all fear of the tribulations and disappointments of this life and also in strengthening me to suffer them and to give thanks to the Lord, Who, as I now believe, has delivered me from such terrible and never-ending torments.[66]

Just as we have noted in the stories of other individuals who have survived NDEs, for Teresa, experiencing the torments of Hell was life-changing—not in the way seeing the Grand Canyon or other momentous sights can be, but in a much more profound way. Thereafter, St. Teresa wanted to live for God and Heaven. And so sin had lost its savor and the devil's grip had loosened. St. Teresa also understood that Hell would have been her fate had she not turned fully away from vice and embraced a life of virtue and prayer.

[65] *Life of St. Teresa*, chap. 32, par. 5.
[66] *Life of St. Teresa*, chap. 37, par. 10.

While she may have experienced Hell only in flashback thereafter, St. Teresa did, conversely, have a very real continuation on earth of her experience of Heaven.

The Transverberation of St. Teresa

St. Teresa's famous transverberation—a word that means being "pierced through the heart"—may be one of the most in-body experiences in all of history's out-of-body experiences. Through a mystical grace, St. Teresa received a "dart of love" from an angel who pierced her heart straight through. She had so desired to be filled with love and zeal for Jesus that, through one of His angels, He deigned to grant her this grace and so to draw her even closer to Him as His bride.

Here is St. Teresa's description of the event from her autobiography. It begins with an insightful survey of the various ways in which the Lord permitted angels to visit her:

> Our Lord was pleased that I should have at times a vision of this kind: I saw an angel close by me, on my left side, in bodily form. This I am not accustomed to see, unless very rarely. Though I have visions of angels frequently, yet I see them only by an intellectual vision, such as I have spoken of before. It was our Lord's will that in this vision I should see the angel in this wise. He was not large, but small of stature, and most beautiful—his face burning, as if he were one of the highest angels, who seem to be all of fire: they must be those whom we call cherubim. Their names they never tell me; but I see very well that there is in heaven so great a difference between one angel and another, and between these and the others, that I cannot explain it.[67]

---

[67] *Life of St. Teresa*, chap. 29, par. 16.

We see in this passage that St. Teresa makes an interesting distinction among the various ways in which angels visit her. The angels mostly appear to her as an "intellectual vision." This time, however, the angel is corporeal and smaller. This presumes that the angels typically appear much larger, as we will see in other accounts of OBEs and NDEs.

Now we'll take a look at the account of the angel sinking a spear into St. Teresa—not unlike the spear that pierced the hearts of Jesus and Mary:

> I saw in his hand a long spear of gold, and at the iron's point there seemed to be a little fire. He appeared to me to be thrusting it at times into my heart, and to pierce my very entrails; when he drew it out, he seemed to draw them out also, and to leave me all on fire with a great love of God. The pain was so great, that it made me moan; and yet so surpassing was the sweetness of this excessive pain, that I could not wish to be rid of it. The soul is satisfied now with nothing less than God. The pain is not bodily, but spiritual; though the body has its share in it, even a large one. It is a caressing of love so sweet which now takes place between the soul and God, that I pray God of His goodness to make him experience it who may think that I am lying.[68]

---

[68] *Life of St. Teresa*, chap. 29, par. 17. Original footnote: " 'The most probable opinion is, that the piercing of the heart of the Saint took place in 1559. The hymn which she composed on that occasion was discovered in Seville in 1700 ("En las internas entrañas"). On the high altar of the Carmelite church in Alba de Tormes, the heart of the Saint thus pierced is to be seen; and I have seen it myself more than once' (*De la Fuente*)."

Note St. Teresa's powerful description concerning the transformation of her soul: "The soul is satisfied now with nothing less than God." It is similar to St. Augustine's famous line from his *Confessions*: "Our hearts are restless, O Lord, until they find their rest in You." But St. Teresa's words strike at something even deeper than that which St. Augustine was communicating. Her words are perhaps the best summation of the effect of (and God's purpose for) NDEs and OBEs. This is the change that overtakes a person: From the moment of such an experience, the affected person begins to abhor sin and to pine for that divine beauty that was so briefly encountered. Past satisfactions and pleasures have now lost some or all of their savor. The person is wrecked for life—albeit in the best way possible.

Of course, St. Teresa is not some wayward soul who survived a motorcycle accident after living a life of wantonness. She was already a mystic, breathing that rarefied air of the saints, when the transverberation occurred. For her, that OBE was a next-level experience.

St. Teresa explains the experience further:

During the days that this lasted, I went about as if beside myself. I wished to see, or speak with, no one, but only to cherish my pain, which was to me a greater bliss than all created things could give me. I was in this state from time to time, whenever it was our Lord's pleasure to throw me into those deep trances, which I could not prevent even when I was in the company of others, and which, to my deep vexation, came to be publicly known. Since then, I do not feel that pain so much.... On the other hand, when this pain, of which I am now speaking, begins, our Lord seems to lay hold of the soul, and to throw it into a trance, so that there is no time for me to have any sense of pain or suffering, because fruition ensues at once. May He be blessed forever, who hath bestowed such great graces on one who has responded so ill to blessings so great![69]

St. Teresa uses such vivid imagery: "Our Lord seems to take hold of the soul and throw it into a trance."[70] This is akin to the "yanking" of the soul out of the body that is frequently described in modern NDEs. St. Teresa's insights on her OBE are so valuable to us because they offer a different perspective on the succession of events when compared with what we see more frequently, for she was no spiritual amateur; rather, she was a master of the interior life. By contrast, God gives many people NDEs or OBEs precisely because those people are focused on carnal desires rather than spiritual goods. Indeed, most of the accounts in this book describe a person's radical changes for the better, such as the men who might easily have been described as prodigal sons and who became priests after their experiences.

Such experiences are, in large part, dramatic because of the great conversions they effect. What's amazing with St. Teresa's account is that, even though she was no prodigal child, her account is nonetheless *dramatic*. For that matter, it is, in fact, one of the most dramatic moments in Church history and even in European history.

The Incorrupt Heart of St. Teresa

Did you know that there is actual, physical proof of St. Teresa's pierced heart?

---

[69] *Life of St. Teresa*, chap. 29, par. 19. The Carmelites keep the feast of this piercing of the saint's heart on August 27.

[70] I am here modifying the original translation a bit.

St. Teresa died in 1582—this time for real—and nine months later, her body was exhumed and was found to be incorrupt, according to the account below:

> The coffin was opened on July 4, 1583, nine months after the interment; they found the coffin lid smashed, half rotten and full of mildew, the smell of damp was very pungent.... The holy body was covered with the earth which had penetrated into the coffin and so was all damp too, but as fresh and whole as if it had only been buried the day before.... They washed the earth away, and there spread through the whole house a wonderful penetrating fragrance which lasted some days.[71]

Not only was her body found without any evidence of decay; something incredible was found in her heart too. There was an astonishing wound in her heart. It was the wound from the angel's spear.

St. Teresa's heart was subsequently removed from her chest, enclosed in a crystal vessel, and reposed in a jeweled silver reliquary in the Carmelite Monastery of Alba de Tormes in Spain. The crystal vessel, on at least two occasions, has *exploded*, as if "incapable of resisting the internal pressure of that extinguished volcano of love."[72]

St. Teresa's incorrupt heart can still be seen today. It has kept its color, and her body remains incorrupt after nearly five hundred years.[73]

---

[71] Auclair, *Teresa of Avila*, 430–431.

[72] Ribera, *Vida de Santa Teresa de Jesus*, 140n2.

[73] An article recently appeared in *Popular Mechanics* describing the recent re-exhumation of St. Teresa's body. Again, she was found to be unchanged from the pictures taken during her last exhumation

St. Teresa's Vision of Heaven

In addition to her vision of Hell, St. Teresa received a vision of Heaven. She wrote that this vision was filled with an indescribable light, which unfolded gradually. She also wrote that Jesus allowed her first to see His pierced hands and then later His radiant face:

It pleased our Lord, one day that I was in prayer, to show me His Hands, and His Hands only. The beauty of them was so great, that no language can describe it. This put me in great fear; for everything that is strange, in the beginning of any new grace from God, makes me very much afraid. A few days later, I saw His divine Face, and I was utterly entranced. I could not understand why our Lord showed Himself in this way, seeing that, afterwards, He granted me the grace of seeing His whole Person. Later on, I understood that His Majesty was dealing with me according to the weakness of my nature. May He be blessed forever! A glory so great was more than one so base and wicked could bear; and our merciful Lord, knowing this, ordered it in this way. You will think, my father, that it required no great courage to look upon Hands and Face so beautiful. But so beautiful are glorified bodies, that the glory which surrounds them renders those who see that which is so supernatural and

---

in 1914. Details were also discovered regarding the suffering she experienced in her life. "We know that the last few years were difficult for her to walk," Fr. Marco Chiesa remarked in a press release. "Analyzing the foot [relic] in Rome, we saw the presence of calcareous spines that make walking almost impossible." Michael Natale, "Nuns Exhumed the Tomb of a Saint Who Died in 1582: Her Face Is Still Stunningly Visible," *Popular Mechanics*, September 11, 2024.

beautiful beside themselves. It was so with me: I was in such great fear, trouble, and perplexity at the sight. Afterwards there ensued a sense of safety and certainty, together with other results, so that all fear passed immediately away.[74]

St. John of the Cross, St. Teresa's friend and contemporary—and a great mystic in his own right—said the following of such experiences of great fear: "In the spiritual passage from the sleep of natural ignorance to the wakefulness of the supernatural understanding, which is the beginning of trance or ecstasy, the spiritual vision then revealed makes the soul fear and tremble."[75]

Note the sublime language that St. Teresa uses to describe not just the sacred face and hands but all glorified bodies:

On one of the feasts of St. Paul, when I was at Mass, there stood before me the most Sacred Humanity, as painters represent Him after the resurrection, in great beauty and majesty, as I particularly described it to you, my father, when you had insisted on it. It was painful enough to have to write about it, for I could not describe it without doing great violence to myself. But I described it as well as I could, and there is no reason why I should now recur to it. One thing, however, I have to say: if in heaven itself there were nothing else to delight our eyes but the great beauty of glorified bodies, that would be an excessive bliss,

---

[74] *Life of St. Teresa*, chap. 28, pars. 2–3.

[75] "Quamvis in principio visiones a daemone fictae aliquam habeant pacem ac dulcedinem, in fine tamen confusionum et amaritudinem in anima relinquunt; cujus contrarium est in divinis visionibus, quae saepe turbant in principio, sed semper in fine pacem animae relinquunt." St. John of the Cross, *Spiritual Canticle*, st. 14, 84.

particularly the vision of the Humanity of Jesus Christ our Lord. If here below, where His Majesty shows Himself to us according to the measure which our wretchedness can bear, it is so great, what must it be there, where the fruition of it is complete!...

But our Lord made such haste to bestow this grace upon me, and to declare the reality of it, that all doubts of the vision being a fancy on my part were quickly taken away, and ever since I see most clearly how silly I was. For if I were to spend many years in devising how to picture to myself anything so beautiful, I should never be able, nor even know how, to do it; for it is beyond the reach of any possible imagination here below: the whiteness and brilliancy alone are inconceivable. It is not a brilliancy which dazzles, but a delicate whiteness and a brilliancy infused, furnishing the most excessive delight to the eyes, never wearied thereby, nor by the visible brightness which enables us to see a beauty so divine. It is a light so different from any light here below, that the very brightness of the sun we see, in comparison with the brightness and light before our eyes, seems to be something so obscure, that no one would ever wish to open his eyes again.

It is like most pellucid water running in a bed of crystal, reflecting the rays of the sun, compared with most muddy water on a cloudy day, flowing on the surface of the earth. Not that there is anything like the sun present here, nor is the light like that of the sun: this light seems to be natural; and, in comparison with it, every other light is something artificial. It is a light which knows no night; but rather, as it is always light, nothing ever disturbs it. In short, it is such that no man, however gifted he may be, can ever, in the whole course of his life, arrive at any imagination of what it is. God puts it before us so instantaneously, that we could not open our eyes in time to see it, if it were necessary for us to open them at all. But whether our eyes be open or shut, it makes no difference whatever; for when our Lord wills, we must see it, whether we will or not. No distraction can shut it out, no power can resist it, nor can we attain to it by any diligence or efforts of our own. I know this by experience well, as I shall show you.[76]

Listen to the beauty of St. Teresa's words. Rarely in the history of human language has the reality of Heaven been so closely approached in words.

Take a moment to reread her words. Let the beauty of what is awaiting us in Heaven, what Jesus has prepared for us, soak in. She speaks of a light that does not wane or dazzle and of a reality so sublime and entrancing that our eyes would never tire of looking at it. By such light, even the light of the sun dims.

If anyone doubts whether Heaven exists, let this written account of St. Teresa's experience prove otherwise.

---

[76] *Life of St. Teresa*, chap. 28, pars. 4, 7–8. "The holy Mother, Teresa of Jesus, had these imaginary visions for many years, seeing our Lord continually present before her in great beauty, risen from the dead, with His wounds and the crown of thorns. She had a picture made of Him, which she gave to me, and which I gave to Don Fernando de Toledo, Duke of Alva." (Jerome Gratian, *Union del Alma* (Madrid, 1616), chap. 5. Whether this painting of Jesus, commissioned by St. Teresa, is still extant is unknown.

5

ST. THÉRÈSE OF LISIEUX

October is an auspicious month for St. Thérèse of Lisieux —and an important month for the Blessed Mother as well. St. Thérèse's feast day is October 1 — the day after her death on September 30, 1897. October 2 was also a significant day for St. Thérèse. It was on that day in 1882 that her sister Pauline entered the Carmelite monastery and that ten-year-old Thérèse Martin — perhaps because the devil could not stand the thought of two Martin sisters entering the monastery and all the future defeats that would mean — fell deathly and mysteriously ill.

In her autobiography, *Story of a Soul*, St. Thérèse describes her illness as the devil's retribution. "This suffering so affected me that I soon became seriously ill. The illness was undoubtedly the work of the devil, who, in his fury at this first entry into the Carmel, tried to avenge himself on me for the great harm my family was to do him in the future."[77]

Our Lady of Victory would ultimately prevail against St. Thérèse's diabolical affliction; this cause of her cure is reflected

---

[77] *The Story of a Soul: The Autobiography of Saint Thérèse of Lisieux*, illustrated, annotated study-guide and workbook ed., ed. Scott L. Smith, Jr. (Holy Water Books, 2021), 44.

in her October feast day, but her healing is not the only great rescue attributed to Our Lady in October.

Nearly four hundred years before St. Thérèse's birth, a monumental battle took place on October 7, 1571—a battle that could forever have changed Catholicism in Europe. October 7 became the feast of Our Lady of the Rosary, originally named Our Lady of Victory. This feast commemorates the Battle of Lepanto of 1571. The whole of Christian Europe joined in praying the Rosary to protect the combined Christian armadas of the Holy League, which were significantly outnumbered by the Muslim fleet. It was a decisive victory for the Church, and Pope Pius V instituted the feast of Our Lady of Victory. This marked the peak of Muslim power and expansion in the Mediterranean Sea.

But this was a very large, complex, almost global event. By contrast, the Little Flower lived her life focusing on her Little Way of doing small things with great love, as Mother Teresa of Calcutta would later say. St. Thérèse's devotion to Our Lady and her miraculous recovery through Our Lady's intercession was like a little flower planted beside the great oak of Our Lady's victory at Lepanto.

In curing St. Thérèse, the Blessed Mother received the title "Our Lady of the Smile." As St. Thérèse wrote in *Story of a Soul,* "It needed a great miracle, and this was wrought by Our Lady of Victories herself."[78]

The Nature of St. Thérèse's Sickness

On October 2, 1882, St. Thérèse's dearest sister, Pauline, entered the Carmelite monastery. After the death of their mother, St. Zélie Martin, Pauline had become Thérèse's second mother. Thérèse

---

[78] *Story of a Soul,* 46.

was only four years old when her mother died; now, with Pauline's departure, it seemed as if she were losing her mother all over again.

Thérèse did not yet know the "joy of sacrifice" and suffering, so her pain at this parting was intense. She wrote: "How can I describe the anguish I suffered! In a flash I saw life spread out before me as it really is, full of sufferings and frequent partings, and I shed bitter tears."[79]

Pauline's entrance into the monastery seemed to cause incurable physical and mental torments for young Thérèse, who would undergo terrible suffering in the months following Pauline's departure.

The sickness began with constant headaches. These intensified as winter approached, leading to shivering, convulsions, hallucinations, pains, and a lack of appetite.

St. Thérèse's doctors, including the psychiatrist Dr. Marie-Dominique Fouqueray, were baffled by her disease.[80] Thérèse's sister Marie, who never left her side through her torments, recalled hearing the doctor's prognosis after observing one of the girl's strange fits. The doctor said there was nothing science could do for the child. No treatment helped.

There was no respite from her torments, except on one day: April 6, 1883. It was the day Pauline received her habit at Carmel. It was also Eastertide.[81] The Little Flower had been suffering for nearly seven months at this point.

St. Thérèse describes this day in her autobiography and makes it clear that there was no merely natural origin to her illness:

[79] *Story of a Soul*, 42.

[80] Dr. Marie-Dominique Fouqueray, "A Strange Illness: The Illness of Thérèse at Age Ten from Easter to Pentecost 1883."

[81] Easter Sunday was on March 25 in 1883, which happened to coincide that year with the Solemnity of the Anunciation.

On reaching home I was made to lie down, though I did not feel at all tired; but next day I had a serious relapse, and became so ill that, humanly speaking, there was no hope of any recovery.

I do not know how to describe this extraordinary illness. I said things which I had never thought of; I acted as though I were forced to act in spite of myself; I seemed nearly always to be delirious; and yet I feel certain that I was never, for a minute, deprived of my reason.

Sometimes I remained in a state of extreme exhaustion for hours together, unable to make the least movement, and yet, in spite of this extraordinary torpor, hearing the least whisper. I remember it still. And what fears the devil inspired! I was afraid of everything; my bed seemed to be surrounded by frightful precipices; nails in the wall took the terrifying appearance of long fingers, shriveled and blackened with fire, making me cry out in terror. One day, while Papa stood looking at me in silence, the hat in his hand was suddenly transformed into some horrible shape, and I was so frightened that he went away sobbing.

But if God allowed the devil to approach me in this open way, Angels too were sent to console and strengthen me. Marie never left me, and never showed the least trace of weariness in spite of all the trouble I gave her.[82]

St. Thérèse's sickness appeared to be supernatural in origin. Though harassed by the devil, she was not possessed. Another one of her sisters, Céline Martin, who later became Sr. Geneviève of St. Teresa, testified to this point. Witnessing her sister's sufferings,

---

[82] *Story of a Soul*, 45.

Céline noted, "Unlike with illnesses caused by the devil, pious objects never frightened her."[83] Demonstrating revulsion to holy or blessed objects is a telltale symptom of demonic possession.

That St. Thérèse was suffering from demonic harassment, however, appears clear. Her cries of distress terrified everyone around her.

St. Thérèse's sister Marie dutifully remained at her bedside. Like the rest of her sisters—Pauline, Céline, Léonie and Thérèse—Marie would also later become a religious, taking the name Sr. Marie of the Sacred Heart. Years later, this same Sr. Marie was asked to provide testimony for the beatification and subsequent canonization of St. Thérèse. Regarding this period, Sr. Marie testified that, although Thérèse never lost her ability to reason, she experienced "terrifying visions that gave chills to all those who heard her cries of distress." She further described that, during some of the incidents, "Her eyes, which were usually so calm and gentle, had an expression of terror in them that is impossible to describe."[84]

St. Louis Martin and the Statue of Our Lady of Victory

One such example of these terrifying visions, described above, was the transformation of her father's hat. Thérèse recalled watching as her father's lumpy, worn hat suddenly morphed into some hideous, menacing shape. Her father, St. Louis Martin—was so disturbed by her reaction to his presence that he began to weep in despair. After half a year of such torments, he was grief-stricken over the fate of his daughter.

[83] Joseph Pronechen, "St. Thérèse of Lisieux Was Miraculously Cured by Our Lady of the Smile," *National Catholic Register*, October 2, 2019, https://www.ncregister.com/blog/st-therese-of-lisieux -was-miraculously-cured-by-our-lady-of-the-smile.

[84] Pronechen, "Miraculously Cured."

Thérèse recalled how her father suffered greatly, thinking that she was going to die. Louis had already lost his wife and four other children. Thérèse said that the Lord might have comforted her father during this time, telling him, "This illness is not unto death; it is for the glory of God" (John 11:4). Of course, if Thérèse had indeed had such awareness, she might also have comforted her father. But she came to the realization after the fact that her father did not know that "the Queen of Heaven was watching faithfully over her Little Flower, that she was smiling upon it from on high, ready to still the tempest just when the delicate and fragile stalk was in danger of being broken once and for all."[85]

In May 1883, Louis gave money to Marie, ever at Thérèse's side, to send for a novena of prayers to be offered at the Basilica of Notre-Dame-des-Victoires in Paris—another connection to Our Lady of Victory—for a cure.[86] Given that the doctors had indicated that they thought that the origin of Thérèse's illness was not natural, it seemed to her father that a miracle would be necessary to restore her health. As Thérèse would later write, "Yes, a great miracle, and this was wrought by Our Lady of Victories herself."

In addition to sending Marie for a novena that day, Louis also brought a statue of the Blessed Mother into Thérèse's room. This would prove to be a pivotal move in her miraculous cure.

This particular statue, which had long been venerated in the Martin home, was a copy of a much-loved statue of the Blessed Virgin Mary created in 1735 by Edmé Bouchardon (1698–1762),

---

[85] *Story of a Soul*, 44.

[86] The Basilica of Notre-Dame-des-Victoires was named by King Louis XIII, who dedicated it to his victory over the Protestants at La Rochelle in 1628 during the French Wars of Religion. It was not named for Our Lady of Victory. Nevertheless, it was the same Blessed Mother interceding for both victories.

one that was later destroyed during the French Revolution. It also closely resembled the image of the Blessed Mother found on the Miraculous Medal, which was first created in Paris in 1832; some biographers of St. Catherine Labouré believe that her confessor, Fr. Jean Marie Aladel, presented a copy of Bouchardon's statue to use as an inspiration for the goldsmith, Adrien-Jean-Maximilien Vachette, who was charged with crafting the first Miraculous Medal.

Moments of relief were rare during Thérèse's strange and prolonged illness. Nevertheless, in those few precious moments that she did feel marginally better, if there were fresh flowers on hand, she contented herself by weaving embellishments for the Blessed Mother's statue. She beautifully described this beloved pastime:

> When my sufferings grew less, my great delight was to weave garlands of daisies and forget-me-nots for Our Lady's statue. We were in the beautiful month of May, when all nature is clothed with the flowers of spring; the Little Flower alone drooped, and seemed as though it had withered forever. Yet she too had a shining sun, the miraculous statue of the Queen of Heaven. How often did not the Little Flower turn towards this glorious Sun![87]

The Little Flower would not droop and wither forever—nor even much longer.

The Novena Concludes on Pentecost Sunday

May 13, 1883, was another auspicious day for Thérèse. Not only was it Pentecost Sunday, but it was one of the last Sundays of the Novena of Sundays that her father had sought from Notre-Dame-des-Victoires. It was also another date of Marian significance, for

---

[87] *Story of a Soul*, 46.

thirty-four years later, Our Lady would appear to the children of Fátima on May 13.

On this rare occasion, Thérèse's sister Marie was in the garden instead of sitting with her little sister. Léonie, however, remained at Thérèse's side.

Thérèse would later describe what happened next: "I began to call: 'Marie! Marie!' very softly … so I called louder, until Marie came back to me. I saw her come into the room quite well, but, for the first time, I failed to recognize her. I looked all round and glanced anxiously into the garden, still calling: 'Marie! Marie!' "[88] When Thérèse continued to be unable to recognize her sister, Marie knelt down in tears at the foot of Thérèse's bed. As she knelt, she turned toward the statue of the Virgin Mary and begged her intercession with all the fervor of a mother who begs for the life of her child and will not be refused.

Léonie, later Sr. Françoise-Thérèse Martin, testified how, at that moment, all three of Thérèse's sisters who were still living at home fell to their knees, filled with hope, as they implored Our Lady to heal their little sister. Marie, when she was later Sr. Marie of the Sacred Heart, testified that she thought this was going to be the final moment of Thérèse's torments before dying. She and her sisters threw themselves "at the foot of the statue of the Blessed Virgin."[89]

Thérèse later wrote how the pleas of her sisters were a storm sent up to Heaven: "That cry of faith forced the gates of Heaven. I too, finding no help on earth and nearly dead with pain, turned to my Heavenly Mother, begging her from the bottom of my heart to have pity on me."[90]

[88] *Story of a Soul*, 47.
[89] Pronechen, "Miraculously Cured."
[90] Pronechen, "Miraculously Cured."

The result of these prayers was both swift and startling, according to Thérèse. She wrote next how the statue of Our Lady responded:

Suddenly the statue seemed to come to life and grow beautiful, with a divine beauty that I shall never find words to describe. The expression of Our Lady's face was ineffably sweet, tender, and compassionate; but what touched me to the very depths of my soul was her gracious smile. Then, all my pain vanished, two big tears started to my eyes and fell silently.... They were indeed tears of unmixed heavenly joy. "Our Blessed Lady has come to me, she has smiled at me. How happy I am, but I shall tell no one, or my happiness will leave me!" Such were my thoughts.[91]

And thus was born the title "Our Lady of the Smile."

St. Thérèse Is Cured

This was not the first time that Thérèse had been saved from the brink of death by a miraculous cure. St. Joseph once protected the baby Thérèse from death and the devil, preserving her to be raised in the holy warmth of Mother Mary. Céline later recounted this early divine intervention. Thérèse was dying of a fatal intestinal disorder that had already claimed the deaths of two Martin children, but Thérèse's mother, St. Zélie, fell to her knees before another family statue, that of St. Joseph. Zélie's pleas before St. Joseph's statue must have mirrored the pleas of the Little Flower's three sisters before Our Lady's statue. Heaven responded, as it so often would when the Martin family combined their prayers, and Thérèse survived.

[91] *Story of a Soul,* 47.

And now, perhaps remembering the work of her most chaste spouse, the Virgin Mary personally appeared to cure the Little Flower. As if the Virgin Mary's apparition was not enough in itself, Thérèse further elaborated on the lasting effects of Marie's prayers:

> [Marie's] prayers had gained me this unspeakable favor: a smile from the Blessed Virgin! When [Marie] saw me with my eyes fixed on the statue, she said to herself: "Thérèse is cured!" And it was true. The Little Flower had come to life again—a bright ray from its glorious Sun had warmed and set it free forever from its cruel enemy. "The dark winter is past, the rain is over and gone,"[92] and Our Lady's Little Flower gathered such strength that five years later it opened wide its petals on the fertile mountain of Carmel.[93]

Not only had the warmth of the Virgin Mary's smile cured Thérèse —that warmth would carry Thérèse all the way to her own entrance into the Carmelite monastery.

Thérèse's vision during this cure had lasted more than forty minutes. It may have felt like just a moment to Thérèse, but she had been transfixed, focused on the statue for a substantial amount of time, as her sisters noticed and would later relate.

After the apparition, Thérèse looked around at her sisters and "recognized Marie; she seemed very much overcome, and looked lovingly at me, as though she guessed that I had just received a great grace."[94]

Marie soon asked Thérèse to reveal what had happened. She fully believed the Blessed Mother had appeared to Thérèse. The

---

[92] Song of Sol. 2:1.
[93] *Story of a Soul,* 48.
[94] *Story of a Soul,* 47.

Little Flower admitted that she "could not resist [Marie's] tender and pressing inquiries." Thérèse waited until she was alone with Marie and told her that she was astonished that Marie knew her secret, even though she had not said a word. Thérèse then divulged what had happened and how the Blessed Mother had smiled at her.

After hearing what St. Thérèse experienced through Our Lady's grace when she was so close to death, do you feel a stirring of devotion to Our Lady of the Smile? If you would like to honor Mary through this particular path, here is the prayer asking for the intercession of Our Lady of the Smile:

Prayer to Our Lady of the Smile

O Mary, Mother of Jesus,
and our gentle Mother too,
with a visible and radiant smile
you consoled and cured
your beloved child, St. Thérèse of the Child Jesus.
We ask you now to smile on us,
amid the troubles of our lives.
May your gentle smile bring light and healing
to the darkness and disease of our body, mind, and spirit.
Instill us with hope and deepen our faith
so that we may enjoy forever
your maternal and enrapturing smile in Heaven.
Amen.[95]

---

[95] "The Healing of Our Lady of the Smile," Society of the Little Flower, January 9, 2021, https://www.littleflower.org/therese-facts/the-healing-of-our-lady-of-the-smile/.

6

POPE ST. GREGORY THE GREAT

I shared in the introduction that, in my experience of finding Catholicism, I discovered that the deeper into it I got, the "further up" and "further in," the more of it there was to find. And this has certainly been true as I have researched these NDEs and OBEs, which are so often experiences of Heaven that have afforded me my own glimpse into eternity. It has been especially true of the subject of this chapter.

As I began researching for this book, I first sought out all the priests I could find who had had NDEs or OBEs, such as Fr. Cedric Pisegna and Fr. Steven Scheier, whom we'll talk about in part 3. Many of them had become priests precisely *because* of these extraordinary experiences they had known. And then I started uncovering saints, such as Padre Pio and Teresa of Ávila, who had some arguably unparalleled NDEs and OBEs—striking in their intensity and revelation. You have already read about St. Teresa of Ávila, of course, and you will read about Padre Pio in the next chapter. But for now, I would like to focus on the story of Pope St. Gregory. When I realized that there was such an individual—a saint who was also a pope *and* a Doctor of the Church who could shed light on what Catholic NDEs and OBEs mean, I might as well have been swept up to Heaven myself.

Who Was Pope St. Gregory the Great?

There are some people, Jesus Christ Himself the foremost example among them, who have had such an impact on history that their character and actions affect us to this day. In Jesus' case, this is true even from a nonbeliever's perspective and also from a purely natural perspective. History itself is numbered according to Jesus' birth. You can hardly turn anywhere without encountering something or someone named for Christ. His name ripples through the centuries and millennia, affecting and determining certain aspects of the lives of people who might not even know His name.

While no one can ever match Jesus in projecting this monumental influence on the lives of countless individuals over the course of history and into our present and future days, Pope St. Gregory the Great was a man whose impact was and continues to be of similar breadth and depth, though to a lesser degree. Have you ever heard of the Gregorian calendar?[96] Or Gregorian chant? This calendar and this type of chant weren't named for a region—there's not, for example, a Gregorian region of Italy. No, they were named for the man.

---

[96] It is a common misconception that the Gregorian calendar created the A.D. and B.C. system. The Gregorian calendar instituted leap year, so the length of a calendar year would match the length of a solar year.

It is generally believed that Dionysius Exiguus, a monk of Scythia Minor, created the A.D.-B.C. system in A.D. 525, counting the years since the birth of Christ. Dionysius's system replaced the Diocletian system, named after the Roman emperor Diocletian, who reigned from A.D. 284 to 305. The Diocletian system used the number of years since Diocletian became the emperor of Rome. The first year in Dionysius's Easter table, "Anno Domini 532," followed the year "Anno Diocletiani 247."

Pope St. Gregory was the final gasp of the Roman Empire's grandeur and greatness. He was born into a Roman patrician family, one of the last, ancient, wealthy families of Rome — a pious family that had already produced two popes.

St. Gregory was also born in the midst of war, plague, and famine. The city of Rome was under a terrible siege in which, according to the historian Procopius, only five hundred people remained alive in the city. The siege starved Rome, and the last Romans were reduced to eating grass and nettles.[97] The great Eternal City was reduced to an empty wilderness, and its treasures were pillaged and ransacked.

Rome died in the childhood of St. Gregory. But it is often at moments like this that something truly remarkable happens in Church history. As Jesus tells us, "Truly, truly, I say to you, unless a grain of wheat falls into the earth and dies, it remains alone; but if it dies, it bears much fruit" (John 12:24). Rome's death bore great fruit, and it rose from the ashes through the efforts of this remarkable and historic man. This is why Pope St. Gregory is known as "the Great."

The Dialogues and "Souls Taken in Error"

Would you believe that not only did Pope St. Gregory the Great write about NDEs but his writings were some of the most popular and widely read in medieval history? Many of these writings are still extant. In fact, more of his writings have survived than those of any other medieval pope, and, indeed, he is the *only* pope between the fifth and the eleventh centuries whose writings and correspondence survived enough to form a comprehensive body of work.

---

[97] Fr. Alban Butler, *Lives of the Saints.*

Of all his works, the most popular during the Middle Ages was *The Dialogues*; it remains widely recognized by scholars to this day.[98] It is a collection of four books of miracles, signs, wonders, and healings done by the holy men of sixth-century Italy. Gregory structured the books almost like an interview between himself and man known in *The Dialogues* as Peter, who was a deacon.

I have highlighted Pope St. Gregory's *Dialogues* because some of their content is directly relevant to our discussion about NDEs and OBEs. It is worth noting, however, that he did not use the term "near-death experience" or anything similar to it. He described the phenomenon of such experiences in a different yet fascinating manner: "souls taken in error." This is in relation to a group of four stories that are recounted in chapter 36 of book 4 of *The Dialogues*. In full, Gregory described the experience as "those souls which seem as it were through error to be taken out of their bodies."

Of course, with the use of such language, Gregory is not accusing God of committing errors or of taking souls in error. Gregory believed such an experience to be highly significant, and not a mistake or an accident that happens without meaning. On the contrary, St. Gregory says that an occurrence such as this "is an admonition" from God.

An NDE is indeed a warning to a person. Similar to the revelations that Dickens's Ebenezer Scrooge experienced in *A Christmas Carol*, an NDE occurs so that the person who lives through it may change his life for the better—in short, to avoid eternal damnation.

[98] John Moorhead, "Taking Gregory the Great's *Dialogues* Seriously," *Downside Review* 121, no. 424 (July 2003): 197–210. Also, "The Figure of the Deacon Peter in the *Dialogues* of Gregory the Great," *Augustinianum* 42, no. 2 (2002): 469–479.

Gregory elaborates on this "admonition" as follows: "For God of his great and bountiful mercy so disposeth, that some after their death do straightways return again to life, that having seen the torments of hell, which before when they heard they would not believe, they may now at least tremble at, after they have with their eyes beheld them." This is like the inverse of Doubting Thomas, who would not believe the good news that Jesus has been resurrected. These people do not believe how *horrible* the bad news really is. Doubting Thomas would not believe until he put his finger in Christ's wounds. Likewise, God, in His infinite wisdom, knew that these survivors would not "tremble" at Hell unless "their eyes beheld [it]."

These glimpses of Hell flow from God's mercy, divine mercy. God is not masochistic. He does not enjoy terrifying His children. He desires to draw us to Himself, to live an eternity in His presence in Heaven. He is literally and mercifully scaring the Hell out of these people. It is a gift.

Plucked by an Angel: The Monk Who Was Saved from Hell

In the fourth volume of his *Dialogues*, Pope St. Gregory tells us what happened to a monk who was thrown into Hell. But before we get into the details of that story, let me stop and ask you something: If you had an NDE or an OBE, would you rather see Heaven or Hell? That's an easy question, right? *Right?* If we were to see all the suffering of Hell, we might respond as Kurtz did in Joseph Conrad's *Heart of Darkness* (and as Marlon Brando did in *Apocalypse Now*): "The horror. The horror."

But what if that was all you needed to scare you straight? To break you from whatever sin ails you or imprisons you? To see the spoils of sin for what they truly are? To taste their true taste?

To see Hell, then, might not be such a bitter pill after all.

St. Gregory provides an account of just such an NDE—that of a monk, Sclavonion, who was thrown into Hell. Sclavonion lived in one of the monasteries founded by St. Gregory himself, with whom he shared this story.

Sclavonion told of another monk named Peter. Together, these two monks lived a penitential life, praying and fasting in a vast desert called Evasa. Peter had been drawn to the ascetic deprivations of the desert after an NDE. What happened was this.

One day, Peter was struck dead by an unknown sickness, and he found himself suddenly surrounded by the "torments and innumerable places of hell." He saw many of the "mighty men" of this world, the famous generals and statesmen, "hanging in those flames" of Hell. He soon found that his own soul was being carried down in the pit to be thrown into the same fire.

But just at the moment he was thrown into the fiery pit, and as he felt the first flames licking at his soul, he was snatched out of the noxious fumes. He realized that he had been saved by an angel; an angel had plucked him from the pit.

Whether it was the monk's guardian angel or even St. Michael the Archangel himself, who had likewise plucked Moses' body from the pit, was not recounted. But Peter did describe the angel appearing in "beautiful attire," and he told Peter he would not suffer him to be cast into such torments. He spoke to him thus: "Go thy way back again, and hereafter carefully look unto thyself, how thou leadest thy life."

These words of the angel are the singular message of every NDE. They perfectly encapsulate, as only the words of an angel could, the spiritual significance of NDEs and OBEs.

After this encounter with his angel, Peter returned to life, awakening from the "sleep of everlasting death." His fellow monks reported that the dead monk's body "little and little became warm."

God gave Peter a most effective "admonition." This is ultimately why Sclavonion found him living as a hermit in the desert. In the tradition of the Desert Fathers, Peter's life of sacrifice was undertaken not just for his own benefit but to assist all souls in their goal of reaching Heaven. This is the purpose of monastic life. Peter bound himself to fasting and watching and silent prayer. His very life and conversation, when the order of grace permitted, spoke to what torments he had seen and was afraid of. So, as St. Gregory wrote, "God's merciful providence wrought in his [temporary] death that he died not everlastingly."

Those Whom Even Hell Cannot Save: The Account of Stephen Not the Smith

Lest we grow too confident in man's ability to change his wicked ways, St. Gregory also provides an account of a heart that persists in evil. "But because man's heart is passing obdurate and hard, hereof it cometh that though others have the like vision, and see the same pains, yet do they not always reap the like profit."

The man whom Gregoy is speaking of here was named Stephen. Unlike the monk Peter, he did not "reap the like profit," for Stephen saw Hell and yet did not change his ways.

This is far from the only account of the hardness of man's heart. Even God's direct intervention in a person's death is not enough for some. "Further up and further in!" The Catholic Church contains a vast wealth of such accounts.

Now, for the details of Stephen's story, which he told directly to St. Gregory, who regarded him as an "honorable" man. He was, according to St. Gregory, wrongly summoned to his death. He was traveling on business to the great ancient city of Constantinople, which was then the capital of the Roman Empire. Due to an unknown ailment, Stephen suddenly fell sick and died.

By a lucky coincidence, there was no surgeon available to "bowel" and embalm him. He lay dead and unburied all day and all night. While his body was awaiting burial, Stephen found himself being carried down, down into the dungeons of Hell. He saw many things. All the sights of Hell were laid before him, things that he had heard about in life, but "little believed"—until then.

At the end of this road through Hell, he found himself waiting upon a judge. It does not appear from St. Gregory's account that this judge was one of the heavenly court or God; rather, it was some hellish bureaucrat. The vast, sprawling, and often dehumanizing bureaucracies of modern government were surely made in the image of Hell. And the hellish ones are just as prone to error as the earthly ones, as you are about to see.

Stephen waited upon this demon bureaucrat for the devil knows how long, but the bureaucrat refused to see him. Eventually, Hell's appointed bureaucrat was forced to admit that Hell had made a mistake. He said, "I commanded not this man to be brought, but Stephen the Smith."

According to no less an authority than Pope St. Gregory the Great, Hell had gotten the man's name wrong! So what ended up happening to Stephen *not* the Smith? He was straightaway restored to life—and Hell provided no note of apology, as you might imagine.

You might also be wondering what happened to the man who was Stephen the Smith. He was a resident of Constantinople, and he died at the very hour our first Stephen was restored to life.

But this is not the end of our first Stephen's story, for remember, he was the man who failed to profit from his tour of Hell's torments. St. Gregory reports that Stephen eventually returned to Rome from his trip to Constantinople, and then he died about three years later. In short, he exchanged one premature death for another, but we don't know many details of his death beyond the fact that it was due to some kind of disaster or widespread plague that affected the whole of the city. St. Gregory refers to "that mortality which lamentably wasted this city (and in which, as you know, men with their corporal eyes did behold arrows that came from heaven, which did strike divers)." What these "arrows that came from heaven" are, regrettably, remains a mystery lost to history.[99]

This same mysterious pestilence would also befall the subject of St. Gregory's next account of an NDE: a soldier. And, as we shall see below, Stephen's ultimate fate is intertwined with the soldier's account.

The Soldier's Account of His NDE

After his death in this mysterious pestilence, the soldier later recounted having a sense of being carried out of his body—as we know now, this fits one of the usual patterns of NDEs. In this state, the solider said that he found himself laying "void of all sense and feeling."

Upon suddenly regaining awareness, the soldier saw an interesting sight: a bridge. A black, smoky river ran beneath it, and issuing from the river was a "filthy and intolerable smell." On

---

[99] Though I suspect St. Gregory means something more literally akin to "arrows," it is possible that this unknown pestilence was the plague of Justinian, which occurred in the middle of the sixth century, 541–549. The Justinianic plague was the first known outbreak of bubonic plague in western European history. The plague struck the Mediterranean at a pivotal moment, just when the emperor Justinian was attempting to restore the Western Roman Empire at Rome. The plague frustrated Pope St. Gregory's and Justinian's combined efforts to build the Church and rebuild Rome at that time. This might be why St. Gregory described the pestilence in supernatural terms.

one side of this bridge lay a far, green country. Pleasant green meadows full of sweet flowers filled the landscape as far as the eye could see. Great companies of men dressed in white filled the green glades and dales.

To the soldier, these companies of men appeared as great armies arrayed across the plains. This place was the reward of those who had shown valor in battle; it was filled with heroes from battlefields throughout history. This was the reality that the pagans half-grasped as Valhalla in the Norse tradition or the Elysian Fields in the Greek tradition. Their last battle cry was being raised aloft through the sweet air. St. Gregory's soldier also provides a pungent description of the smells of this place. A fragrant odor "did give wonderful content to all them that dwelt and walked in that place."

Beyond the green fields and victorious armies, this soldier could discern multitudes of individual mansions, "all shining with brightness and light." There was one house of special magnificence and sumptuousness. It glinted in the light, for its bricks were made of gold. Whose it was, he knew not.

But closer to the riverbank, the quality and disposition of the houses were mixed. The river's rising, stinking vapors touched some but not others. Meanwhile, souls crowded the bridge and its approaches. Many souls desired to cross over it, but not all were permitted. Those who attempted the crossing were subject to a trial.

This was the manner of the trial: If the wicked attempted to cross, they fell into the dark, stinking river. The weight of their sins dragged them down. The just, who were unhindered by sin, "securely and easily passed over to those pleasant and delicate places."

Amid the masses of people, it appears, the soldier was able to discern those whom he knew in life, for he reported seeing a man named Peter, who had been the steward of St. Gregory's family, as well as a priest and our first Stephen, *not* the Smith.

Peter, the Steward of the Pope's Household

Peter, the steward of St. Gregory, had died four years ago and had since received the just rewards of his unworthy deeds in life. The soldier found him "thrust into a most filthy place," bound there to a great and inescapable anchor of iron.

The soldier asked why Peter was bound in iron. This was the punishment, the soldier was told, for the cruelty Peter had demonstrated in life. Both the soldier and St. Gregory were well aware of Peter's lack of mercy toward his subordinates in life. Whenever Peter had any occasion to punish another, he whipped them sadistically, enjoying their pain—and never out of a desire to teach them obedience.

Peter's cruelty was now being revisited upon him many times over. Sadly, the soldier reported no knowledge of how long Peter's torments would last, whether forever or merely a purgatorial span. Peter's reputation in life was of such a kind, it seems, that the soldier was unconcerned with the duration of Peter's torments.

The Priest

Next, the soldier watched a priest cross the bridge. The soldier had known this noble priest in life, and he saw him rightly pass over the bridge without fear or trepidation. The priest's feet were sure and secure along the bridge, as "he [had] lived in this world sincerely."

The Last Account of Stephen *Not* Smith

The soldier also witnessed our first Stephen and shared this final accounting of his soul. Just as he was about to cross the bridge, his foot slipped. The soldier saw half of Stephen's body hanging below the bridge, and then a truly ghastly sight emerged from the murky depths of the river.

"Terrible men" erupted from the inky folds of the river. They latched onto Stephen's legs and ankles with claws and teeth, and they began dragging him down, down into the depths. The soldier saw Stephen as he clung desperately to the bridge. His head and torso suddenly lurched downward. It was only a matter of time before his grip would fail him.

But then, a bright light illuminated Stephen's desperate struggle. White-clad and beautiful persons appeared above Stephen, grasping him above the waist and arms, bearing him upward. There was a momentary struggle when the soldier dared not breathe, lest the least wayward motion snap Stephen's tensioned body into two miserable halves.

At just this moment, the soldier was restored to life. St. Gregory ends the account with the soldier "not knowing in conclusion what became of [Stephen]."

The Meaning of Stephen's Bitter Struggle

What was St. Gregory's understanding of the struggle over Stephen's soul—the two sides fighting a terrific game of tug-of-war over his hapless form? Gregory interprets that there was a battle being waged within Stephen. Whether the battle was being fought internally or externally is not a relevant inquiry, as, along the bridge, the internal is unveiled and the two are as one.

Within Stephen, St. Gregory tells us, "the sins of the flesh did strive with his works of alms." Stephen's love of giving alms in life was being weighed against the wages of his sins. The alms were drawing him upward, while his impurities sought to drag him down into the filthy stream.

St. Gregory further explains: "Apparent it is, that both he loved to give alms, and yet did not perfectly resist the sins of the flesh, which did pull him downward: but in that secret examination of the supreme judge, which of them had the victory, that neither we know, nor he that saw it."

Note, this was a *secret* examination. St. Gregory explains that neither we nor the soldier are permitted to see the final outcome of Stephen's trial by the "supreme judge." The cliff-hanger ending was intended by God, who had permitted the soldier's vision of Stephen and everything else that he saw.

St. Gregory also reiterates that God had specially prepared Stephen for this moment through Hell's prior mistake. In fact, Hell's mistake might have been God's work all along. God, says St. Gregory, had attempted to spare Stephen from this seemingly interminable back-and-forth along the bridge. Yet, after his own NDE, Stephen failed to take appropriate measures in life to prevent this uncertain outcome. St. Gregory is clear: "Yet most certain it is, that the same Stephen, after that he had seen the places of hell, as before was said, and returned again to his body, did never perfectly amend his former wicked life, leaving us in doubt whether he were saved or damned."

Until the mysterious "arrows of heaven" began raining down on Stephen, he likely thought there was still time to change his ways and break himself from his carnal addictions. This should be a sobering note to us all. We know neither the hour nor the day when our time will come to cross the bridge of death.

St. Gregory concludes these accounts with another sobering note: "When any have the torments of hell shewn them, that to some it is for their commodity, and to others for their testimony: that the former may see those miseries to avoid them, and these others to be so much the more punished, in that they would not take heed of those torments, which they both knew and with their eyes beheld."

That is, an NDE is both a blessing and a curse. God intends these "miraculous visions" to be a blessing and an opportunity for people to amend their lives, to be the "Ebenezer Scrooge" turning point, so to speak. St. Gregory adds another element to this, however, one that is rarely discussed. To see these torments of Hell and yet not act accordingly is a curse one brings on himself. Worse torments may yet befall them. As St. Gregory says, they are "to be so much the *more* punished, [if] they would not take heed of those torments."

The Meaning of the Golden Mansions

Some conclusions are obvious from the soldier's account, the "miraculous vision," as St. Gregory describes it. The beautiful green plains and golden mansions, for instance, are the landscape of Heaven. It is uncertain, however, whether the filthy places beyond and beneath the bridge were Purgatory or Hell. It might have been that Peter was bound forever, in which case he was damned in Hell. Or his torments might instead have been of a temporary nature, and he was ultimately awaiting salvation.

St. Gregory engaged in the sixth-century equivalent of a question-and-answer session at the end of this portion of *The Dialogues*. His interlocuter was the fictional Peter—an ominous pseudonym, given the torments of Peter the steward just described.

The first question that this fictional Peter poses is to wonder why the heavenly mansions should be made of bricks of gold? What possible need would we have of such a metal in the next life? St. Gregory answers that these gold bricks of the soldier's heavenly mansion represented the almsgiving and other virtuous works that the soldier gave in his life on earth. Heaven kept an accounting of all of these good deeds of his. As the soldier's time for a true death had not yet come, his mansion was still in the process of being built. The golden bricks were being carried to the soldier's home by the old and the young, both girls and boys, men and women. These were the people whom the soldier helped in his life, whether he knew it or not. For, as St. Gregory says of this detail: "[This,] by which we learn that those to whom we shew compassion in this world, do labour for us in the next."

St. Gregory also adds another account of a man named Deusdedit, perhaps another title like "soldier," whose house in Heaven was mysteriously constructed only on Saturdays for the day of his good works in life.[100]

The building of our future heavenly abode with golden bricks is also mentioned in Scripture, specifically in 1 Corinthians 3:10–15, which provides us with one of the clearest descriptions of Purgatory found in the New Testament:

> According to the commission of God given to me, like a skilled master builder I laid a foundation, and another man is building upon it. Let each man take care how he builds upon it. For no other foundation can anyone lay than that which is laid, which is Jesus Christ. Now if any one builds on the foundation with gold, silver, precious stones, wood,

---

[100] St. Gregory's description of Deusdedit's home: "There dwelt also hard by us a religious man, called Deusdedit, who was a shoemaker, concerning whom another saw by revelation that he had in the next world a house and building; but the workmen thereof laboured only upon the Saturday. Who afterward enquiring more diligently how he lived, found that whatsoever he got by his labour all the week, and was not spent upon necessary provision of meat and apparel, all that upon the Saturday he bestowed upon the poor in alms at St. Peter's church: and therefore see what reason there was, that his building went forward upon the Saturday."

hay, stubble—each man's work will become manifest; for the Day will disclose it, because it will be revealed with fire, and the fire will test what sort of work each one has done. If the work which any man has built on the foundation survives, he will receive a reward. If any man's work is burned up, he will suffer loss, though he himself will be saved, but only as through fire.

The Greek word for *fire* in the last line above is transliterated as *puros*; this is actually the word from which we derive our word *Purgatory*. This whole Scripture passage describes the construction of our lives as a building, the foundation of which is Jesus Christ. When we are burned up through this purifying fire, the "*gold, silver, and precious stones*" of our good works will remain. The "wood, hay, and stubble" of our sins will be burned off through purification.

Apparently, this soldier had performed many corporal works of mercy in life, and this golden edifice was his "reward," along with Heaven itself.

The Meaning of the Bridge and the Two Sides of the River

Peter next asks St. Gregory why some houses were touched by the stinking vapors and some were not. He also asks what is meant by the bridge and the river. St. Gregory explains that, from the bridge, we learn that the path that leads to everlasting life is very straight and narrow. It is entirely likely that the bridge is, as we describe it today, the tunnel. There are at least three reasons why we might think this: the physical size of it, its location, and the signature event of each location.

First, there is a physical correspondence between the narrowness and straightness of the bridge and that of the tunnels that are described in NDEs and OBEs. Second, there is also a geographic correspondence, as both the bridge and the tunnel lead to Heaven. Third, similar events are reported as occurring in both locations.

The stinking river, St. Gregory continues, which runs beneath the bridge, signifies "the filthy corruption of vice in this world [that] doth daily run to the downfall of carnal pleasure." St. Gregory also describes the meaning of the stinking vapors—that is, why were some of the houses touched with the fumes and some were not? He explains that this represents all of those many people who, despite doing many good works, still stink of carnal sins and pleasures. What is perceived as a stench in the next life exists as our disordered inclinations and vices in this life. The stench is not perceptible as such on this side of the veil.

Gregory references a passage from Job to further explain this point. The stink of the pleasure of the flesh was perceivable to Job, so much so that he described the wanton and carnal man saying, "Worms be his sweetness" (Job 24:20, Douay-Rheims). On the other hand, Gregory says that the stinking vapors avoid those who "preserve their heart free from all pleasure of carnal thoughts," for a free and pure heart can better see the "brightness of true light." Carnal pleasure, however, darkens the intellect and the sight.

Gregory also summarizes the Beatitudes, specifically the beatitude that assures us that the pure in heart shall see God: "For the more pleasure [the soul] hath in the inferior part, the more darkness it hath in the superior, which doth hinder it from the contemplation of heavenly mysteries."

St. Gregory further substantiates his point by referencing the stinking vapors of brimstone that rained down on Sodom along with fire (Gen. 19:24). Both rained down, according to Gregory, that "fire might burn them, and the stench of brimstone smother and kill them." Because their flesh in Sodom burned with "unlawful" and unholy love, it was God's judgment that their flesh should burn. The "unsavory smell" was added that "they might know that they had, by the pleasure of their stinking life, incurred the sorrows of eternal death."

On this "unsavory" note, St. Gregory ends the portion of his *Dialogues* in which he discusses NDEs. His ancient account of them is certainly unique. It is a bridge of sorts between the various biblical NDEs presented herein and the more modern accounts, from St. Teresa of Ávila to the present. As a bridge, these accounts are important because they add to our understanding of the fact that NDEs are not new. The human race has experienced this phenomenon throughout its history, indeed throughout all of salvation history.

7

PADRE PIO

St. Pio of Pietrelcina, affectionately known as Padre Pio, reminds us that God is not finite—He is not limited. We can try to put limits on the number of miracles God can work in our lives, perhaps thinking something along these lines: God has already done so much for me—I can't expect any more. But Padre Pio shows us that this way of thinking is foolish.

In just such a way, we might be inclined to think that NDEs and OBEs are such a rarity that, if someone were to experience such a thing, surely it would happen only once in a lifetime, or perhaps twice at the very most. But just as God defies our instinctive tendency to expect limitations, so, too, does Padre Pio's witnessing defy any definition of any NDE as a once-in-a-lifetime event. For saints and mystics such as Padre Pio, NDEs and OBEs were common experiences. They were not one-time visitors to a supernatural realm, unschooled tourists of the Divine but, instead, were so familiar with it—either through their own repeated encounters with it or through the confidences of individuals who came to them for understanding and guidance—that they might well be master tour guides and interpreters of such things for the rest of us. And indeed, Padre Pio's experience with NDEs is not limited to his *own* experiences; it is well documented in numerous cases that he appeared in other people's NDEs.

In one instance, Sara Luce, an Italian woman who was deathly ill in the hospital, awoke to a strange reality: Padre Pio was at her bedside, prepared to travel with her to a place of engulfing, warm, white light.

There is also the testimony of Padre Pio's spiritual son, Fr. Jean Derobert. This French priest was shot dead in the Algerian War and swept up into Heaven with Padre Pio as his guide, protector, and intercessor—and came back to tell the tale.

Fr. Jean Derobert's NDE

Meeting Padre Pio

Padre Pio had twenty-five men and women whom, over the course of his life, he adopted as his spiritual children. They were privileged to be under his particular care and protection, and many of them were set on the path to sainthood through his direction. One such young man was the French seminarian Jean Derobert, who was studying in Rome when he came to know Padre Pio. He was a unique addition to Padre Pio's spiritual family, as the vast majority of Pio's adopted children were not just Italian but were *local* Italians, hailing from Pietrelcina or other villages and towns close by Pio's home. They were also primarily laymen, with the exception of some religious women. Derobert's encounter with Padre Pio, which occurred during a trip he made to visit San Giovanni Rotondo, was auspicious from the beginning; when Derobert first happened to go to him for Confession, Padre Pio dramatically revealed to him his sins that he had not acknowledged due to his insufficient examination of conscience. He also humbled him in revealing to him, during that same confession, proof of the existence of his guardian angel, which he previously had not been convinced of.

That's the short version of how they first became acquainted, but it's worth getting into the details. First, it's important to know that, during much of his lifetime, Pio's reputation in Rome was not good. He had been subjected to many false accusations in the 1920s and was about to be victimized further under the papacy of John XXIII. Many in Rome considered him at best deluded, at worst a con man. But, as they often do, the simple folk of the Italian countryside knew better.

Bearing these preconceptions in mind, Derobert was perhaps a little smug upon meeting the simple Capuchin friar. But Pio cut through this fog of vanity immediately, and Derobert's boldness evaporated in the confessional. For one thing, Derobert immediately forgot what he wanted to confess. He realized his mind had utterly failed him, and he was dumbstruck.

This was no matter to Pio, though, who went about plying his trade as normal, scouring the young man's soul with surgical precision. In Pio's confessional, it was he, not the penitent, who performed the examination of conscience. Pio began peeling back the layers of sins that Derobert had hidden, even from himself. He revealed that there was extensive spiritual rot that Derobert had missed by sheer negligence. Here are Derobert's own words about what happened in that confessional:

> With tears in his eyes, [Pio] showed me the gravity of certain acts … gravity that, to tell the truth, had never occurred to me. But upon hearing these things from the mouth of Padre Pio, they took on their true dimensions. "This is serious.… It's serious!" And he wept. I was in great difficulty, especially since everything he said was true. He also gave me precise details that I had totally forgotten about. Sometimes one acts on reflex, with no sense of guilt whatsoever.[101]

[101] "Padre Pio and the Seminarian's Guardian Angel," *Il Nuovo Arengario*, trans. Francesca Romana, reprinted in *Rorate Caeli*, October

Derobert was no longer there to amuse himself at what he had supposed would be the silly antics of the poor Capuchin friar; he was humbled when he remembered that he had come to try to spot chicanery or fraud in Padre Pio. He had come to San Giovanni parroting those in the Vatican who suspected Pio of deception. Now, somewhat bewildered after receiving absolution, he was about to receive one of the most important lessons of his life. This is where the story of his unbelief in his guardian angel comes into play.

When Padre Pio asked him if he believed in his guardian angel, Derobert was taken aback. Guardian angels? Surely the idea of such creatures was an outdated belief for pious and medieval peasants. But for a well-educated seminarian from Rome to believe in such things in this day and age? *Hardly.* After what he had just experienced in Pio's telling him his own sins, though, Derobert dared not laugh out loud. Instead, he awkwardly chirped the first silly thought that came to mind. He said, "Um, I've never seen him!"

The next thing he knew, Derobert's cheeks were stinging and his ears were ringing. Pio had slapped him, perhaps even on behalf of the boy's angel. And then Pio said, "Look carefully. He is there … and he is very beautiful!"

Derobert whipped his head around, expecting to see a mass of feathers and beaming halo: "I, for sure, saw nothing, but the Father had the expression in his eyes of one seeing something. He was not looking into empty space. 'Your Guardian Angel is here

9, 2022, https://rorate-caeli.blogspot.com/2022/10/padre-pio-and-seminarians-guardian-angel.html; unless otherwise cited, all of the quotations in the story of Fr. Derobert, recounted in the following pages, come from this source.

protecting you! Pray well to him!' Padre Pio's eyes were luminous, reflecting the light of my Angel."

Derobert could see the light of his angel, but only as reflected in Pio's eyes. He never again trifled with his guardian angel and even went on to write several books about our guardian angels.

Death in Algeria

The year of Derobert's first meeting with Padre Pio, 1955, was a turbulent time in French history. A long way from the glorious victories of Napoleon, France was now merely trying to avoid humiliation in the international community; its colonial territory, Algeria, was waging a war of independence.

Three years later, in August 1958, Fr. Derobert was serving in the French Army Health Services, and he had been assigned to Algeria. He knew that something momentous was about to happen because he had just received a letter from his spiritual father, Padre Pio. Whether it was something good, bad, or otherwise, he did not know; he just knew that when Pio sent him a letter assuring him of his prayers and support, it was time to buckle up.

Pio had previously sent him letters before Derobert's examination at the Gregorian University in Rome and again when he left for the army. And now, Pio had written to him following his assignment to the fighters in Algeria.

Fr. Derobert, who would later become Abbot Derobert, would write of his experiences in Algeria that followed on this "warning" from Padre Pio. (This letter would later become part of the documentation and proceedings for Padre Pio's canonization). Here is how he begins his "summary on the topic of the protection with which he was gifted" by Pio: "One night, a commando of the FLN [Algerian National Liberation Front] attacked our village. I was immediately restrained and placed in front of a door with five other soldiers; and that's where we were shot."[102]

That's how Fr. Derobert died. He was executed by the FLN with five other soldiers. Of course, it is strange to hear him write so matter-of-factly about his own death, since we know he was alive while writing it.

He narrates what happened next, providing a detailed account of his last thoughts—or rather, of his first thoughts as a dead man. First, he notes the strangeness of not thinking about his mother and father. He was an only child, and his thoughts often turned to his parents. Nevertheless, he was overwhelmed with the joy and anticipation of "going to see what was on the other side."[103]

As Fr. Derobert was approaching the "light," he suddenly remembered that he had just received, even that very morning, a note from Padre Pio. On this note, Padre Pio had written only two lines: "Life is a constant struggle but it leads to the light."[104]

Pio had underlined the second half of that line two or three times. It was as if he already knew what was coming.

Derobert next experienced the first in the sequence of characteristics common to NDEs—that is, disembodiment: "I immediately had the experience of a disembodiment. I saw my body next to me, fallen and bloodied in the midst of my comrades, who were also dead."

Derobert's NDE follows the typical sequence closely. He experienced the tunnel next: "I began a curious ascension through a

---

[102] Jean Derobert, *Padre Pio: Transparent de Dieu*, quoted in Patrick Theillier, *Near-Death Experiences Examined: Medical Findings and Testimonies from Lourdes* (New York: Crossroad, 2017), "Sixth Testimony: Shot!," translated from the French.

[103] Derobert, *Padre Pio.*

[104] Derobert, *Padre Pio.*

kind of tunnel." This is where Derobert breaks with the normal pattern. Before he reaches the intense light and joy, his ascension and tunnel experience broaden to include other experiences: "Many known and unknown faces emerged from the fog that surrounded me. At first, these faces were somber; they were faces of people who did not have such a good reputation, sinners lacking in virtue. As I went up, the faces I saw became more luminous."

Derobert's description here is uniquely Catholic. The faces transition from somber to radiant. If there were only two available options for the dead—Heaven or Hell—there would be no somber faces. These are the faces of Purgatory, awaiting entrance into the light.

The Glorified Body

The next section of Derobert's account details his growing tactile, sensory, and atemporal awareness.

> I was astonished to find out how I could walk … and I told myself that, in my mind, I was already outside of time, I had resurrected. I was able to see all around me without turning around.… I was also surprised that I was not feeling any of the wounds inflicted by the bullets that were shot at me … and I understood that they had entered my body so fast that I was able to hardly feel anything.

Let us unpack this extraordinary paragraph. Derobert was conscious of many things that normally get glossed over. First, he realizes that he is "outside of time." This seems to be more of a description of what is gone, i.e., time, than what this new timelessness feels like. It was the same thing with pain. His experience of painlessness, at this point, is more about what's gone—the sensation of the bullets and the bullet holes—than what's new. Next, he realizes that he can perceive everything around him without turning his head. Imagine if he had poor vision in life. He would have slowly noticed that he could see without glasses too. All of these descriptions from this passage regarding his temporal and spatial awareness may fit within a single category of experience: resurrection.

What I mean by that is that Derobert is describing experiencing something remarkable, something mysterious that we just do not receive a lot of information about: *the glorified body!* Derobert is experiencing his own glorified body, as we will all experience at the final resurrection.

Canonically, much of our knowledge of the glorified body flows from descriptions of Jesus' resurrected body. We know such things as that He could walk through walls[105] and that He still bore the wounds of His earthly torments,[106] but we don't know what that will mean for each of us in the final resurrection. By God's power, each of our souls will be reunited with the same body that it had inhabited during earthly life—but a glorified body, differing from the earthly body as the plant differs from the seed, as described by St. Paul (1 Cor. 15:37–38).

Derobert's improved—*glorified*—eyesight seems to prove what St. Augustine theorized on the matter: "Those eyes [namely, of the glorified] will therefore have a greater power of sight, not so much to see more keenly, as some report of the sight of serpents

---

[105] "On the evening of that day, the first day of the week, the doors being shut where the disciples were, for fear of the Jews, Jesus came and stood among them and said to them, 'Peace be with you'" (John 20:19).

[106] "Then he said to Thomas, 'Put your finger here, and see my hands; and put out your hand, and place it in my side; do not be faithless, but believing'" (John 20:27).

or of eagles (for whatever acuteness of vision is possessed by these creatures, they can see only corporeal things) but to see even incorporeal things."[107]

Derobert next describes how he visited many places, moving at the speed of thought. His thoughts finally turned to his parents. He found himself at his house in Annecy, in his parents' room. They were sleeping. He tried talking to them, but they were unable to hear him. He did, however, note that a particular piece of furniture had been moved. When he later wrote his mother, he asked her why she had moved the furniture. She replied in surprise, "How do you know this?"

Fr. Derobert next moved with the speed of thought to his old friend and mentor, Pope Pius XII. He found himself in the papal apartments. The pope was in his room. He had just gone to bed. Fr. Derobert next describes something remarkable. Unlike his visit to his sleeping parents, he was able to communicate with the pope, despite his disembodied state. This was, perhaps, not the pope's first visit of this kind. Fr. Derobert describes his exchange with the pope: "We spoke through the exchange of thoughts, since he was very spiritually attuned."[108]

As Derobert's description indicates, the glorified body can also be present in many locations or times at once. This is confirmed by what we understand of Christ's glorified body as well, though on a far grander scale. For example, "Christ's glorified body can simultaneously be in heaven and on many altars."[109]

---

[107] *De Civ. Dei* 22, 29, quoted in St. Thomas Aquinas, *Summa Theologica* I, q. 12, art. 3, ad 2, trans. Fathers of the English Dominican Province (London: Burns Oates and Washbourne, n.d.).

[108] Derobert, *Padre Pio*.

[109] Bernhard Blankenhorn, *Bread from Heaven: An Introduction to the Theology of the Eucharist*, ed. Chad C. Pecknold and Thomas Joseph

Derobert also describes communicating with the living. Some people on earth, like Pope Pius XII, can communicate with the saints in Heaven. One can only imagine how many heavenly souls are trying to communicate with us and trying to help us while we are completely ignorant of it.

Derobert's experience reinforces what little we already know about the glorified body, while also giving us a uniquely human perspective of the eternal experience that we are all yearning for.

Intense Light and Joy

Derobert's account of the next steps in his NDE is full of fascinating details, focused on his encounter with a mystical light and also with his having an intense sense of joy:

> I pursued my ascension up to the point where I found myself in a beautiful scenery wrapped in a soft blueish light.... There was no sun, "since the Lord is their light," as it was said in Revelation. I saw thousands of people, all at about thirty years old, but I met a few of them who I had known when they were alive.... One of them died at the age of eighty ... and she looked as if she was thirty.... Another died at the age of two ... and she was the same age as the others.

Derobert is now beyond Purgatory. He is surrounded by the light and beautiful scenery of Heaven proper, and he confirms what St. John describes seeing in the book of Revelation concerning the Heavenly Jerusalem: "And the city has no need of sun or moon to shine upon it, for the glory of God is its light, and its lamp is the Lamb" (Rev. 21:23).

White, Sacra Doctrina Series (Washington, D.C.: Catholic University of America Press, 2021), 207.

Derobert also describes the ages of people in Heaven—that is, the ages of their glorified bodies. St. Thomas Aquinas and St. Augustine both believed that man, upon rising again, would attain a "youthful age," which Augustine defined as beginning about thirty years old.[110] This was based on the apparent age of Jesus after the Resurrection. Derobert's record of his NDE certainly falls in line with this theory.

This should be a beautiful image to anybody who has lost a child, especially a young child or even an unborn child. Even if a child dies before birth, it appears that he or she will nevertheless attain to the age of about thirty. He or she will have lived a *full* life, by some mysterious gift of God.

Fr. Derobert concludes this account of his NDE by stating that he "left this 'paradise' with many extraordinary flowers that [he] had never known down below." In other words, the graces from his NDE were extraordinary, even impacting those who read it.

A Different Ending

At this point in an NDE, a person typically experiences a review of his entire life, perhaps has a meeting with loved ones, and then makes some sort of decision to return to his life—albeit changed forever.

However, this is not the sequence of events that Fr. Derobert relates. Instead, he reaches another level of Paradise, going deeper into that realm. At this point, he becomes a "drop of light," and he sees that he is surrounded by other drops of light. He somehow perceives their identities: Sts. Peter, Paul, and John, as well as other saints. Then he becomes aware of certain lights that are

---

[110] *De Civ. Dei* 2, as in St. Thomas Aquinas, *Summa Theologica*, Suppl., q. 81, art. 1, s.c.

greater than all the others: "Then, I saw Mary in her full radiance and beauty; she met me with her ineffable smile. . . . Jesus was behind her, looking spectacularly beautiful. And behind them was an area of light that I knew was the Father, and I dove head on into it."

If Derobert was given the option to make a decision, he did not decide to return to life but to "[dive] head on into" the presence of God Himself. It is also worth noting at this point in his account that the Virgin Mary's appearance makes this NDE uniquely Catholic. Not only is she present in "full radiance and beauty," but her unique place among the lights and luminaries of Heaven is also established. She is greater than any other heavenly light, save God Himself. At this point, visiting Heaven without noticing her seems implausible at best. She is too bright to miss. And then there is Mary's "ineffable smile," as Fr. Derobert puts it. This may remind the reader of another NDE, that of St. Thérèse of Lisieux and her healing encounter with Our Lady of the (ineffable) Smile.

The ending of the NDE is, at Fr. Derobert describes it, "brisk." The descent is seemingly far more rapid than the ascent was. "There," as he dove head on into the Father, was something more than pure joy: "There, I felt a total fulfillment of everything I could ever have desired. . . . I experienced perfect happiness . . . and briskly, I found myself back on earth with my face in the dirt and in the middle of my comrade's bloodied bodies."

What a contrast! From "total fulfillment" to a face smeared with dirt and the blood of his friends. He had survived the tragedy, the senseless bloodshed of war, but his comrades had not.

He found his clothing riddled with holes, though his body was not. Although he was smeared with streaks and globs of congealed blood, he realized he was not physically wounded.

When Fr. Derobert's superior, Commander Cazelle, saw him, Cazelle cried, "A miracle!" And that, while true, made a poor summary.

Padre Pio's Response to Fr. Derobert's NDE

You may be wondering: If Padre Pio had written to Fr. Derobert because he knew what was coming, what did Pio say when he next saw his spiritual son in the flesh? And where was Pio during Fr. Derobert's NDE? Thankfully for those of us who are curious, Fr. Derobert includes this detail in his NDE account.

Fr. Derobert describes his first visit with Padre Pio after being liberated from the army. Padre Pio appeared from a distance in Saint-Francis Hall and beckoned Fr. Derobert to come closer. Padre Pio offered Fr. Derobert "a small sign of affection," as was their custom. Then Padre Pio told Fr. Derobert, " 'Oh! You really took me for a ride this time! But what you saw, it was really beautiful, wasn't it?' And he stopped at that."[111]

Couldn't Pio be just a little more verbose this *one* time? In his characteristically taciturn manner, no words were wasted.

What a "ride," as Pio put it. It seems that he accompanied Fr. Derobert for his entire journey, even though Derobert never described seeing him. With that likelihood in mind, we are left to wonder: Had Pio not undertaken this journey with his spiritual son, would Derobert's journey have been very different?

For this reason, we pray that a watchful guardian like St. Pio or St. Joseph will accompany us, too, as we undertake our final journeys — or, as in Fr. Derobert's case, something less than our *final* journeys.

[111] Derobert, *Padre Pio.*

Part III

NEAR-DEATH EXPERIENCES OF PRIESTS AND LAYPEOPLE

8

FR. CEDRIC PISEGNA

When the idea came to write a Catholic collection of NDEs, I was, as I mentioned at the beginning of this book, still suspicious of the phenomenon. I told God that, if He wanted me to do this, He would need to provide me with material. Outside of my own family, I had never heard of a Catholic NDE. I wasn't even sure if the Catholic Church countenanced such experiences.

Enter Fr. Cedric Pisegna. Fr. Cedric's OBE, which shared so many essential details with the characteristics of an NDE, was the first such explicitly Catholic experience that I had ever heard of. In fact, his book *Death: The Final Surrender* was basically the beginning and end of the entire Catholic NDE bibliography. All of the quotations in the following pages, unless otherwise cited, are taken either from this autobiography or from an interview that he graciously granted to me as I was in the process of writing this book.

Responding to a Call

"My evening began simply enough," Fr. Cedric explains.[112] It was July 1977, and he was a twenty-year-old college student. Though he had been raised Catholic, he had fallen away from the Church

---

[112] Fr. Cedric Pisegna, *Death: The Final Surrender* (self-publ., 2021), 61.

and was living the life of your typical college student: a swirl of girls, partying, and the rest.[113]

He had just finished his sophomore year and was at his parents' home in Massachusetts on summer break. He was lying on the living-room floor and watching a Red Sox game.

Fr. Cedric's experience follows the typical pattern and includes some of the typical characteristics of an NDE. What's strange, however, is that he was not at all "near death," at least that he knew of.[114] While watching a Red Sox game in the seventies and eighties could certainly be a *harrowing* experience, it was not quite "near death."

He explained that that time in his life "had been a summer of searching," and he referred to himself as a "spiritual misfit." About a year earlier, he had begun waking up asking, "What is all this?" Questions like these hovered over him like the cloud of an unrelenting storm—thoughts such as, "I'm not happy. I feel like I'm missing something. I know there is more to life than what I have. I'm not satisfied." These thoughts were pervasive and unrelenting, despite the fact that young Cedric was not seeking them out. He was not willfully or otherwise embracing some sort of existential funk. In fact, on this day, he was just trying to watch baseball and enjoy his summer.

Recalling this time years later, with the benefit of age and perspective, he explains what was happening to him: "A wonderful truth about God is that he will make you hungry even though you don't know what you are hungry for."

---

[113] Personal interview with the author.

[114] This kind of experience is better classified as an out-of-body experience (OBE).

Adopting an "if you can't beat 'em, join 'em" mentality, young Cedric began to try to appease his conscience by reading the Bible. Now, as I mentioned earlier, Cedric had ceased practicing his Catholic Faith. Even Christianity was not an "ongoing reality" in his life. Nevertheless, he sought out the Bible as a source of truth. He wanted to know what answers Jesus had to the questions that were plaguing him. And, as he began to pray and read Scripture, he found that faith began to well up within him. As he described it, "faith emanates from the deep recesses of the heart," and just so, he began to develop a relationship with God. Remembering the growth of faith at this time, he reflected: "The seed of faith will grow of itself when it is nourished by prayer, God's word, obedience and worship. Little did I know, but each morning, as I woke up and prayed and read the Bible, faith was growing in and of itself."

As St. Paul preached to the Athenians, God created them so "that they should seek God, in the hope that they might feel after him and find him" (Acts 17:27). For about nine months, a reasonable period of gestation, Cedric was searching diligently for God.

Death Is a Passage We Can't Practice

Fr. Cedric's seventh-inning stretch took an unusual turn. As he was watching the Red Sox on that summer afternoon, he began drifting off to sleep. And then suddenly, he "felt [himself] being pulled down a passageway." Although he was conscious and aware of what was happening, he found he had no power to resist it. He explains that many of us will experience this same kind of movement when we die: "This 'pulling, or magnetic propulsion' is exactly what will happen at the mysterious moment of our death. Death isn't a cessation of life, but a passing, a transition to supernatural life. There will be a release, a letting go of the body and a transcendent movement to God."

Fr. Cedric repeats this many times for emphasis: He wants us to know that death is not primarily defined by the end of life, but by the beginning of something new. It's hard for us to grasp this truly and deeply if we have no firsthand experience of such a thing, but hopefully this book is giving you the vicarious experience of it! Among other things, as he relates what happened that day, Fr. Cedric also wants to ease the fear of an impending *nothing*. He tells us that this fear could not be further from the truth.

Additionally, he tells us that we shouldn't worry about not knowing how to die: "You didn't know how to be born into this world, but it happened by God's design. Your death has been decreed by God also."

He has a point. I had nothing to do with the success of my birth, and neither did anybody I know have anything to do with the successes or difficulties of their own births. This is not to say that we do not have a responsibility to live well and to overcome sin by participating in God's grace and the sacraments with the goal of preparing ourselves well for death and the eternity that awaits us beyond. Of course we do. But there is no skill needed for dying.

The Tunnel and the Veil

To help us better understand the tunnel experience of NDEs and OBEs, Fr. Cedric uses some earthly examples. He describes the tunnel as being like a "wormhole," or at least how science fiction has depicted wormholes. This also helps describe the sensation of being pulled through and floating through a floorless tunnel.

When he was a teenager, he worked at an amusement park, and he likens the tunnel to one of the rides: "One of rides had a catwalk that went right through a swirling circular tunnel. That is the best way to describe what was happening to me. I felt as if I was being pulled through a tunnel or canal of some sort. I didn't see it, but I somehow sensed it was round about me. It was a definite passageway."

This is one of the clearest, most tangible analogies for the tunnel that I have come across. If you have ever been through one of those amusement-park tunnels, you know how disorienting the experience can be.

It seems strange to Fr. Cedric now, but, at the time, he didn't want to go through the tunnel. He said he was being "pulled against [his] will, and I didn't have the strength to resist."

When asked to describe what exactly it was that was pulling against his will, he responded: "Just as the force of gravity is a law we can't resist, at the moment of our death, there will be a supernatural law. We will gravitate to God. I did try to resist, but no matter how I fought it, I was still pulled through. I felt powerless, helpless, and out of control."

Such appears to be the force of God's will beyond the veil. People may struggle with God on this side of the veil but not in death. Not at all. The truth of God's existence suddenly becomes irrefutable, unassailable. What is sinful or not, what is just or unjust—all debate ceases. If only we could live like this *now*. So many of us are utterly confused. If we could just keep this reality before us always, we could avoid so many mistakes. Unfortunately, we are easily distracted on this side of the veil.

As Fr. Cedric describes it, God is aware of every little thought, motive, and intention in our lives. Every imagining, every deed, is under His scrutiny. And yet we live as though each one of us were the only judge of our actions, the only arbiter of truth.

Fr. Cedric describes the intolerable oddness of reality for the atheists, the materialists, and the empiricists: "Somehow God has created a world where it seems like we are alone and no one knows our thinking. The way God has ingeniously designed the world, faith and doubt, virtue and vice, love and selfishness can play their roles. Only a vastly intelligent God could create a massive universe like this, and yet you can still choose to doubt that God exists."

Sadly, we often act like irrational animals rather than children of God. Jesus often likened the world to a poorly tended vineyard—and Isaiah spoke about how God would lay waste to His vineyard, "remove its hedge," "break down its wall," and "it shall be trampled down" (Isa. 5:5).

How much better would the earth, the vineyard, and all its souls be tended if there was no doubt that God existed or that He is watching us? Fr. Cedric answers this (emphasis added): "A child sure that he is being watched will most likely behave his best, but one unaware of being observed will allow his true self to come to the fore. I am sure of this: *we are not alone*."

How many of us misbehave, thinking that we can sin privately? If only we truly understood that there is no such thing as a secret sin, what sins might be avoided? How many souls might be saved? Not that God is watching and waiting for us to make mistakes, but He is always present, always ready to provide His grace and strength. How many souls despair of loneliness? If only they knew, intimately, that they are not—were never—alone.

The Psalms tell us that God "know[s] when I sit down and when I rise up; thou discernest my thoughts from afar" (Ps. 139:2). This "afar" doesn't mean a great distance. It means beyond time and beyond the veil, which may, nevertheless, be infinitely close. St. Augustine says it best: "God is closer to us than we are to ourselves."[115]

As Fr. Cedric was going through this experience, he made a mental note:

[115]St. Augustine, *Confessions*, bk. 3.

Everything on earth seems so safe and secure. Things are definitely not what they seem. There is so much more than meets the eye. Life on earth is illusory. What I mean is that when we think or act or live we feel like we are the only ones present. But just beneath the surface of our thoughts and consciousness, there is a whole new transcendent reality. We live on the tip of the iceberg, as it were.

This is the sacramental nature of reality. Every sacrament is an outward sign, instituted by Christ, of an invisible reality. There are cosmic battles being waged just beyond the veil. We are "surrounded by so great a cloud of witnesses," not to mention angels and demons (Heb. 12:1). In his OBE, Fr. Cedric was coming to grips with these sublime truths. He rightly likens our impression of reality to an iceberg, most of which lies hidden beneath the veil of the ocean's surface.

The Summons

In retrospect, as he told me when we spoke together, Fr. Cedric understood his OBE as a "summons" from God Himself.

Jesus tells us in John's Gospel (emphasis added), "No one can come to me unless the Father who sent me *draws him*; and I will raise him up at the last day" (John 6:44). This verse means that God will draw people to salvation through Jesus, and, sure enough, Fr. Cedric found himself being drawn to the Father: "I found it coming true literally as I was drawn like a magnet to Jesus."

There was never any doubt where Fr. Cedric was headed. This is not to say that Fr. Cedric's salvation was guaranteed. He was simply assured of reaching God the way that those in a crashing airplane are assured of reaching the ground: "I instinctively knew where I was going. I was transcending to God. This had never happened to me before, but it is just something instinctive: I just knew I was on the way to God."

Fr. Cedric had little faith at that time. But now, something odd was about to happen: "Strangely enough, what was pulling me through that passageway was my faith! As I was being pulled forward, I remember thinking, 'Oh no, I believe!' I said 'Oh no' because I was being pulled to an imminent meeting with God.... I also said 'Oh no' because I knew I was about to come before God. I was overwhelmed. Yes, God is loving, but are you ready to come before him right this second? Trust me, you will be afraid."

Not only was Fr. Cedric coming to grips with the reality of God at that moment, but He was also coming to an understanding of the reality that God is astounding and ineffable. More than that, God's presence can be *terrifying*. Awe and fear of the Lord are a gift of the Holy Spirit.

The "sense of transcendence" permeated Fr. Cedric's OBE. Time stood still. He was beyond time and "moving in a new realm," and he was conscious of being summoned to the Beatific Vision.

Does Everybody Pass through the Tunnel?

Fr. Cedric states that the passageway experience is nearly universal. He elaborates on the universality of the "death moment":

This passageway is the first thing you encounter at the moment of release. When a person's body is old, sick, or damaged by an accident, there is a departure at the moment of death. Your body will eventually deteriorate, and you will need to leave it. Your consciousness, your soul, literally vacates your body and begins its journey toward God.

Fr. Cedric argues that this "passageway" or "tunnel" experience is the soul leaving the body. And it is not only that; he also says that it is the beginning of the soul's journey toward God.

This is not a just blur of movement. "At the moment of your death," Fr. Cedric explains, "you will be very aware." He also remarks on the ease and imminence of the experience: "You will have a new awakening, a new consciousness. This movement through the tunnel will occur naturally without your knowing how. It will not take long at all. As I said before, your encounter with Almighty God will be imminent. You will instinctively know what is about to happen, but there must be this 'passing' or transition first."

You know this already, but now and again it's important to remember that your soul never dies. Even in Hell, the soul is alive. That's why Hell is such a tragedy. Fr. Cedric describes why the soul is eternal: "We are made in God's eternal image. God has put eternity in our hearts. That which makes you, your conscience, your consciousness, your personhood, will be preserved and transformed."

Scripture speaks of the "new heart" we will receive. Your body will die, but you will live and spend eternity either in Heaven or Hell.

Fr. Cedric believes a universal "tunnel" or "passageway" experience is involved in this transition. We will "all journey through [this tunnel] at the moment of our death." This passageway is part of "passing away." It is part of the transition between this life and the next. Why should we all leave this life through a tunnel? Fr. Cedric explains that we also all entered the world through a tunnel—our mother's womb:

It's interesting that when we are born into this world, we pass through a tunnel: our mother's womb. No one knows how to be born; it happens naturally. When we are born into the next world, we will all journey through another tunnel. Don't worry about not knowing the way. All of us will go through this passageway instinctively and naturally.

We see this sort of symmetry elsewhere in theology. For example, St. Louis de Montfort gives similar reasoning for why the Virgin Mary is "the surest, easiest, shortest, and most perfect" path to Jesus.[116] This is so because Jesus came to us through the Blessed Mother; naturally, then, the Blessed Mother is the prototypical and best path to Jesus.

Fr. Cedric describes the tunnel as the "womb of eternity."[117] Just as we were born into time originally through our mother's womb, at our death we will be born again into eternity.

Hesitating in the Face of the Light at the End of the Tunnel

Fr. Cedric discovered that the oft-repeated saying "There is light at the end of the tunnel" is true: "Every time I drive through a tunnel such as the one under the Boston harbor or through downtown Mobile, Alabama, it brings to mind vividly that experience. I am writing here about the very moment of our death! God allowed me to remember and share with you."

Maybe this is the real reason why my children hold their breath when passing through a tunnel—maybe because, on some

---

[116] In *Preparation for Total Consecration to Jesus through Mary*, St. Louis de Montfort says, "There is no surer or easier way than Mary in uniting all men with Christ."

[117] This experience of timeliness is somewhat paradoxical for a living person. Even though time appeared to stand still, Cedric noticed that a half hour had passed by the time his soul returned to his body.

instinctive level, they know that we won't be using our lungs anymore when we travel through that final tunnel. Or maybe they're just being kids!

Fr. Cedric also remembers trying to resist the tunnel. Why would he fight against going to God? you might ask. He answers this question:

> I am used to being in control and fear the loss of control. Powerlessness is exactly what I experienced then: the complete loss of control. I had no say in it but I knew where I was going. In some ways it was like the take-off roll of an airplane. There was no turning back and no way out. I had to surrender to what was occurring to me. I hated the feeling of being out of control, but I didn't have the strength to resist because I was drawn down that passageway by a power much greater than myself. The pull was impossible to resist.

Fr. Cedric makes it clear that he was resisting the loss of control. It should be noted that this is not same thing as the loss of free will; it is about "surrender," as Fr. Cedric says above, to God's will. Ever since the Fall, this kind of complete surrender does not come naturally to man. Some of the saints are able to reach such surrender in this life. Most of us, however, need Purgatory to get to that point, and we thank God for it. At this point in Fr. Cedric's life, he was only beginning to learn about surrendering to God's will. He had only just begun down the path to holiness.

Fr. Cedric provides another reason for his hesitancy. He did not feel prepared to come before the presence of God: "I knew instinctively where I was going. I was about to face God, and I wasn't ready." Fr. Cedric compares his dread to what St. Paul described in his Letter to the Hebrews: "It is a fearful thing to fall into the hands of the living God" (Heb. 10:31).

Fr. Cedric speaks about how the tunnel he experienced was not unlike tunnels of man's construction. Like Boston's Ted Williams Tunnel—to return briefly to Boston and the Red Sox!—the end of a tunnel can be a blinding experience. For Fr. Cedric, the light at the end of the tunnel is more blinding than any earthly light: "Before I knew it, even though I didn't know how, I was at the end of the tunnel. Suddenly, I found myself in the presence of God himself."

Here, Fr. Cedric's OBE moves into the "intense light" and "life review" phases that are common to so many NDEs and OBEs. The light that issues from God is the light of illumination—the illumination of conscience. This kind of light peers deeper into your being than any X-ray or CT scan.

Fr. Cedric describes this moment, a moment that will come for us all and that he recognizes as the particular judgment described by the Church:

> At the moment of your death, there will come an immediate encounter with God. You will meet your maker. You will remember where you have come from. Your soul came from and will return to God. . . . It is crucial that you live in such a way that you will be happy when you discover who you really are: your true self! Either you will be justified or bring shame to your eternal soul.

Fr. Cedric describes this moment as the sudden end to our long pilgrimage of life. Some will be justified, and some will not. Some will feel intense joy (another NDE characteristic), while those who have not proven themselves worthy will feel "great shame."

Fr. Cedric remembers that it was "God Himself who said you must be justified." At the time, he didn't even know what the word *justified* meant: "I had to come back and look it up, but I *knew* what it meant ... in that moment." Maybe he did not understand the theological definition of *justification*, but it was still clear to him what God meant by the word.

"I thought I wasn't ready," Fr. Cedric explains. "I needed virtue, and I didn't have any. I needed good works, and I didn't have any. And God was giving me another chance." He further discerned that "God was calling me to the Catholic Church to make a difference."

Bathed in Light: The Glory of the Beatific Vision

Despite all his attempts to resist His summons, Fr. Cedric was now standing before His Creator, before the throne of God.

After the tunnel, young Cedric encountered his true self and much, much more. He found himself "bathed in light":

> One day every person who has ever lived will stand before God. I definitely had the sense that I was standing. What I encountered when I stood before God was glorious and electric. I wasn't allowed to see a form, but what I did see was light—I literally saw the light! It was as if I were looking at the sun with my eyes closed, yet even more brilliant. God is a pure, living luminescent light.

With your eyes closed, have you ever faced directly toward a sun so bright you can almost see the red capillaries in your eyes? Such an experience can give us the barest hint of the "living luminosity" that Fr. Cedric was being immersed in. And indeed Father explains that he wasn't allowed to see the light with "open eyes, because nobody can see the face of God and live" (see Exod. 33:20).

He also describes a physical quality to the light; the light seemed to "embrace" him physically. Can you imagine light that is so bright you can *feel* it? Not feel the *warmth* of the light, but feel the *light itself*? His description of the intensity of the light is also unique in its detail.

It is fascinating that, despite all this sensory overload, Fr. Cedric had the distinct feeling that he was standing. He doesn't remember what he was standing on or in, whether he was barefoot or in sneakers—only that he was standing.

John 1:5 states, "The light shines in the darkness, and the darkness has not overcome it." 1 John 1:5 states, "God is light and in him is no darkness."[118] Fr. Cedric's experience provides insight into these verses: The light is alive. Many who have had NDEs describe God as merely a "Being of light" at this point, but Fr. Cedric's account goes beyond that: "I didn't just see the light; the brightness bathed and embraced me. I knew the light was alive. Somehow, even though I couldn't 'see' clearly, I knew I was in close proximity to God. I simply knew I was right before and very close to God."

The brightness of the light seems to obscure everything else for Fr. Cedric. He cannot answer questions such as "How big is God?" or "What does God look like?" or "What does God's face look like?" He wasn't "allowed," as he describes it, to see these features.

Fr. Cedric experienced God not only as a "Being of light" but also as a Being of glory: "In addition to the brightness and luminescence, there was an overwhelming glory. The glory was moving upwards quickly through me and was also alive."

The Hebrew word for *glory* is *kavod* (כבוד), meaning "importance," "weight," "deference," or "heaviness." Primarily, *kavod* means "respect," "honor," and "majesty." Glory is an attribute of God's power, majesty, and magnificence. While we typically might not think much of the nuances of God's glory, Fr. Cedric's experience reminds us that glory is much more than what we can

---

[118] It is interesting that verse 5 of both 1 John 1 and John 1 describe light in these similar ways.

understand of it from this Hebrew word. God's glory is *alive*. And not only that, but the glory of God is the *what*, or *who*, that raises the dead to life.

As we read in Romans (emphasis added), "We were buried therefore with him by baptism into death, so that as Christ was raised from the dead *by the glory of the Father*, we too might walk in newness of life" (6:4). Jesus was raised from the dead by the "glory of the Father," and we, too, will be raised from the dead through Him. One day, our deceased bodies will be vivified and quickened by this absolute power, by the glory of God!

Fr. Cedric describes his encounter with God's glory in amazing sensory detail:

> God's glory is not just something I observed; it was an electricity and a pleasure or ecstasy that I felt. That I felt the glory is an understatement. I was fully immersed in it. God's glory is a rhythmic, powerful, continuous surge that ran all through me. I could even see it. With light as the background, I could actually see thick horizontal lines consistently and constantly running upwards through me! One example I can think of that describes this is … the waves that flow through a large U.S. flag when it is windy. We even call our flag "Old Glory."

Fr. Cedric likens the waves of God's glory to the rippling waves of Old Glory—a beautiful comparison. It is notable that God's glory, despite the blaze of light, is still visibly distinct from His light.

It was also during this experience of God's glory that Fr. Cedric believes he received the Holy Spirit, for, as he relates it, his experience of God's glory continued even after his OBE: "When I eventually returned to my body, I continued to feel this glory, only to a much lesser degree. We are all familiar with goosebumps and the chills that can run up and down our spine. I came to discern that this pleasant 'prickly' feeling is actually the glory or comfort of the Holy Spirit who lives in us."

Perhaps many of us have felt this sensation when we experience God's presence. For instance, when we receive an amazing insight from a homily, when we notice a coincidence that was no coincidence — a "Godincidence," as we say — we might feel this same sensation, this rippling of God's glory up and down our bodies.

Fr. Cedric's encounter with glory is clearly a description of the Beatific Vision. But what is the Beatific Vision? It is the sight of God face-to-face, the essential bliss of angels and men. The Council of Florence defined the Beatific Vision as the central experience of Heaven:

> The souls of those who after receiving baptism have incurred no stain of sin whatsoever, or who after incurring such stain have been purified, in the body or out of the body ... are at once received into heaven and clearly see God Himself as He is, in three Persons and one substance, some, however, more perfectly than others, according to the diversity of their merits.[119]

Scripture speaks of this vision as the reward of the just. "When he shall appear," St. John says, "we shall be like him, for we shall see him as he is" (1 John 3:2). Similarly, St. Paul contrasts seeing "through a glass darkly" with seeing God "face to face," which is reserved for the life to come (1 Cor. 13:12, KJV).

---

[119] *Decret. unionis.*, quoted in William E. Addis and Thomas Arnold, *A Catholic Dictionary* (New York: Catholic Publication Society, 1887), 68.

Fr. Cedric describes the overwhelming sensory experience of the Beatific Vision:

God is immensely glorious and the waves of glory were constant and breathtaking. God's omnipotence is connected to this strong power. I was standing before Almighty God, the creator of the universe! I somehow saw myself: I had the biggest smile on my face I have ever had. I was experiencing pure bliss and ecstasy. Pleasure was running all through me. . . . I was standing before the throne of God! I was experiencing the rapture all humans seek all our lives, the joy for which we were made. God's presence is the ultimate satisfaction for which we long. What I experienced was an actual taste of the beatific vision for which we are all heading.

The "pure bliss and ecstasy" that Fr. Cedric conveys is enough to make even the martyrs forget the pains of life. As St. Paul describes it, "For this slight momentary affliction is preparing for us an eternal weight of glory beyond all comparison" (2 Cor. 4:17).

Fr. Cedric's experience of pure joy and pleasure demonstrates why our pursuit of pleasure is doomed on this side of the veil:

God's honor became my honor. God shared his honor and dignity with me. I was able to receive it as his child. After having experienced such pleasure, I realized this is why we aren't happy on earth. Our hearts are made for God, not for the cheap facsimiles earth offers. More than contentment, I was finally happy. The triumphant victory and honor given Jesus because of the Cross was generously shared with me.

God wants to share His inexhaustible glory with everyone. According to the Psalms, God "hast made [man] little less than

God, and dost crown him with glory and honor" (Ps. 8:5). God has destined *all* of us for this. As St. Paul says, "And those whom he predestined he also called; and those whom he called he also justified; and those whom he justified he also glorified" (Rom. 8:30).

This experience of God's glory and the Beatific Vision did not end with Fr. Cedric's OBE: "I came to understand through my [experience] that the same glory I encountered in God's presence was now mine to enjoy daily through the person and presence of the Holy Spirit who dwells in me. I sense this glory to a lesser degree on Earth, but nevertheless God's glory still thrills me. This is the comfort or consolation of God's Spirit."

This is important for us to bear in mind, as most of us have not had an NDE or an OBE. This ecstasy of God's glory, albeit to a lesser extent, is available even in *this* life, on *this* side of the veil. It may be significantly more subtle, such as the goosebumps that Fr. Cedric explained above. God's consolations, in whatever form, are widespread in this life, and they are available to all of us through prayer and the sacraments all the time.

The Glory of God Forever?

I often wonder what it will be like to experience God's presence *forever*. This is Heaven—the same experience Fr. Cedric described, but without end. How can one's experience be endlessly enrapturing? My mind might wander a bit more than other people's. Maybe not. But I can imagine no single pursuit on earth that can hold my attention *forever*.

This is sort of its own answer. God's glory, the light of the Beatific Vision, is such that this singular experience *can* satisfy all the desires of our hearts forever. Let the immensity of that thought sink in.

Ponder this reality. The entertainment industry spends billions of dollars annually to hold our attention, but, at best, it creates just a shadow—and sometimes a very dark shadow—of the only thing that can truly captivate us: God's presence.

I would add just one word to St. Augustine's almost-perfect quotation: "Our hearts are restless until they find their rest in You"—*forever*. Fr. Cedric also describes what this all means in the context of forever: "One of the greatest delights of heaven will be that we will experience waves of God's glory forever.... I have had many happy experiences in my life, but none have ever made me completely happy. Standing before God, finally, I had complete happiness."

What does "complete happiness" mean? Fr. Cedric says "happiness is always polluted" on this side of the veil. Our earthly experience of "complete happiness" is typically the relief from suffering or stress: the end of a war, reuniting with a lost family member, completion of a long-sought-after goal, the end of terrible pain. But the "complete happiness" of God's presence is purely the giving of something wonderful, not the loss of something terrible. It is wholly a positive, not the absence of a negative.

"Possessed" by God

Fr. Cedric describes this positive experience of God as something more than just being released from our earthly shackles: "RIP: Rest in Peace. We usually think that will be rest from labors. But there is much more. Resting in God means rest from the anxieties, stresses, fears and distress of life here on earth. Rest as well as peace is the absence of negative thoughts, but more than that, it is the flooding of the positivity of God."

Are you still worried, like me, that your thoughts will wander, even before the Beatific Vision? After all, even in adoration before the Blessed Sacrament, my mind still wanders. Fr. Cedric addresses this too: "I know that many are distressed because of distracting thoughts and evil imaginings that pop into our minds when we don't want them to. We are all plagued by fear, anxiety, worry that torment us. Such thoughts will not occur in God's presence."

This is somewhat reassuring, but without my thoughts, even the tormenting ones, will I still be me? How does that work? Fr. Cedric describes this ecstasy as a process of thinking anew. The word *ecstasy* literally means to "be beside oneself." "As I stood before God embraced by light, clothed in glory, and reveling in the bliss, I noticed that I couldn't really think the way I usually do."

A glorified body means a glorified brain too, right? One of our primary experiences of sin is the darkening of the intellect. Fr. Cedric relates what happens at the illuminating of the intellect.

What I mean is that here on earth we can choose to think certain thoughts. For example, if I want to remember a golf game I played recently, it is easy to do. I simply choose to think about it and I remember. Or if I want to engage in self-reflection and notice how I feel, I am able to do so simply by thinking about it. But when I was in God's presence, I remember that I was so full of God and his peace that it seemed like I had lost the ability to choose my thoughts. I was possessed by God!

Unfortunately, we are more familiar with possession by the devil and his minions than we are with "possession" by God. In full bodily demonic possession, a person "blacks out" and the demon takes possession of the person's mind, thoughts, and body. The person's free will is temporarily gone or severely diminished. "Possession" by God is the light to this darkness, the ecstasy to this horror. It is a "white out," not a blackout.

But still, what does it mean to lose "the ability to choose [our] thoughts"? Do we lose ourselves, if we lose our thoughts? Is our human essence obliterated? Fr. Cedric elaborates a bit further: "I was aware, conscious and simply reveling in the moment. I believe we will be able to choose our own thoughts in heaven, but I was so close to the radiant throne of God that I was unable to think independently."

Compare this description to the times when you have experienced breathtaking beauty. Whether it was an experience of nature's glory, of art, of beauty in the Mass—what happened? We describe beauty as being "arresting." We can be "swept away" by beauty. This is the experience of beauty seizing our thoughts. Our thoughts are no longer "independent," as Fr. Cedric describes, but dependent on the beauty as it carries us away.

Now imagine you are beholding not a mere glimmer of God's beauty, but the source of all beauty itself. Can you imagine how all-enveloping that would be? In God's presence, our minds do not wander *away* from God. They wander—they *run*—*to* God.

> Don't let being possessed by God scare you [Fr. Cedric says]. In this world, being human involves many negative thoughts such as fears, anxieties, bad memories, regrets, stress, sins, etc. The battlefield with the devil is our minds. Many deal with depression, despair, loneliness and panic. We won't be able to think of such things anymore. Instead, we will be "beside ourselves" and be renewed in our minds. We will think God's thoughts and know his ways. We will be totally his. We will still be a distinct soul and our own unique self, but very Godlike.

Can you imagine no longer being enslaved by negative thoughts? If you have experienced the hostile takeover of your brain by depression, blessed are you, for your relief in Heaven will be exquisite.

If you are being constantly attacked by impure thoughts or some other pervasive, habitual sin, can you imagine the relief that Heaven will bring?

As Fr. Cedric says above, "The battlefield with the devil is our minds." Heaven is the end of the battle. As St. Paul wrote, "Oh death, where is thy victory?" (1 Cor. 15:55).

"It's Scary"

Fr. Cedric's experience has hopefully shown you that God's love is anything but "scary." Yet Fr. Cedric ends and summarizes his encounter with the following:

> As I stood before God, bathed in this passionate love, I distinctly remember thinking, "He loves me so much it's scary." Scary is a strange adjective to use about love, I know, but I was overwhelmed with the intensity and longing of God's love. God actually longed for me! Human language doesn't suffice, but some words I thought of to describe God's attraction towards us are: infatuated, jealous of and obsessed with. It was almost as if God needed to love me.

As I wrote in the introduction, NDE accounts often conclude with a reflection on the paltriness and insufficiency of words. Here, again, we reach the limits of human language. We should respond to this with reverence for the glory of God.

Two Experiences?

There are two other common characteristics of NDEs and OBEs that are in evidence in Fr. Cedric's account. First, his life was forever changed by this experience. It was because of his OBE that he became a priest, and he has spent his life sharing the beauty of his experience with others.

Incredibly, Fr. Cedric not only returned to his body, but he also returned to Heaven. That's right; Fr. Cedric experienced *two* OBEs, and the two experiences were exactly the same. Fr. Cedric said he was once asked why he thought this had happened twice. He replied:

> I believe the second one was to affirm the truth of these experiences so that, years later, when I reflect back on what happened to me, the fact that I had two, not just one, dissolves any doubts regarding the veracity of the experience. The second time was a further absorption of God's love as well as a verification of the truth of the experiences.

Fr. Cedric explains this in another way, one he admits is far from perfect:

> When the first plane hit the World Trade Center on 9/11, everyone thought it was an accident. But when the second plane hit, everyone knew it was on purpose. Similarly, the first [OBE I experienced] was no dream or incidental happening, but on purpose for a great purpose. The second again verified the truth of what happened to me. They were both of God's design.

Fr. Cedric's faith has been fortified throughout his life by these experiences. He knows they were not for him alone. He was meant to share them with others—with you. After all, his encounters are about the greatest mystery: what happens at the moment of our death.

9

FR. STEVEN SCHEIER

Fr. Steven Scheier, unlike Fr. Cedric, did not become a priest because of his NDE. He was already a priest—just not a very good one.

He was ordained in 1973 and had been a priest for twelve years when everything changed.

I say that he was "not a very good" priest, but he was actually esteemed in those first eleven years. He himself used that word, *esteemed*, because it was the only way he knew how to measure his success. He was more concerned with what his brother priests thought of him than he was with serving God's people, with being a shepherd.

People thought he was a good priest, but only because of his way of hiding, because of, as he put it, a "sugar coating for everything that I was doing which was wrong and lacking."[120]

It was a trap of sorts. While he would go to his brother priests for practical help with various parish needs, he would never go looking for spiritual aid for himself. "It's not done," he explained. For one thing, it would mean losing the esteem he had so carefully cultivated in an honest, humble admission of the fact that he needed real help.

---

[120] Quotations from Fr. Steven in this chapter come from his interview with Mother Angelica on *Mother Angelica Live*, April 15, 1997.

"Deep down," Fr. Steven says, "I knew that I was not doing what I should be, that I was not the priest that I should be."

Then, the day came that changed everything.

Trauma on the Highway

It was October 18, 1985. Fr. Steven was stationed at Sacred Heart, a small parish in Fredonia, a town in southeast Kansas. Fredonia is almost ninety miles outside Wichita, and the one major road between them is Highway 96, which has no shoulders and is heavily traveled by eighteen-wheelers.

That afternoon, Fr. Steven was traveling back from Wichita, where he had been visiting with a brother priest. For some reason, the road that day was especially full of heavy traffic and big rigs—and Fr. Steven collided head-on with a pickup truck carrying three other people.

"Thank God no one was killed," he said afterward—but this was not entirely accurate, for Fr. Steven himself was launched from his vehicle and suffered deep lacerations across his skull. His scalp was torn off the entire right side of his head. The doctors would later tell him that, due to the nature of the trauma he suffered in being thrown out of his car, the right side of his brain was partially sheared off. Most of the brain cells along that side of his brain were obliterated.

He was barely conscious and almost unresponsive as he lay at the crash scene. A Mennonite nurse who had witnessed the accident stopped to try to help while she waited what seemed an eternity for the ambulance to arrive from Eureka.

The nurse later recounted Fr. Steven struggling to pray the Hail Mary, as he passed in and out of consciousness. She tried to help him, but she didn't know the words. One thing she did know: It looked as if the scalping was the least of his worries. Fr.

Steven's neck had been broken when he hit the ground. It was a C-2 break—that is, a break in the second cervical vertebrae. In grisly parlance, this is known as the "hangman's break."

Usually, such a break is caused by a violent hyperextension of the neck vertebrae due to blunt upward force to the chin, as from hitting the steering wheel or the end of the rope during a hanging. Oftentimes, the windpipe is also crushed, and the person dies by asphyxiation. If Fr. Steven had landed so that his head had turned to either side, he would have suffocated. Thankfully, the nurse was there to hold his head in her hands—his life in her hands—like an image of the Blessed Mother, despite the fact that she didn't know the words to pray with him.

When the EMTs arrived, they carefully moved Fr. Steven into the ambulance and took him to the closest hospital, a rural facility back in Eureka that was, quite frankly, unequipped to treat the severity of his injuries. The emergency doctor in Eureka confided to his sister, who was a nurse there, that there was little he could do to help the priest. He sewed Father's scalp back to his head and prepared him for helicopter transport to the bigger and better hospital back in Wichita.

Father was unconscious for all of this and would not learn the details until much later. From his perspective, one moment he was driving on Highway 96, and the next moment he was back in Wichita in a hospital bed—on some level, at any rate. But during the intervening time, he was very much somewhere else, as we will soon see.

Trickles of the news of his accident reached Fr. Steven's parishioners, and they quickly became desperate for more information. That night, one of his parishioners figured out which hospital he had been taken to and then called the trauma unit in Wichita. The nurses in Wichita shared with him that the doctors were giving

Fr. Steven only a 15 percent chance of survival. This dire news started an avalanche of prayers for his healing. His own church, Sacred Heart, opened its doors. People came all night to pray the Rosary. But that was just the beginning.

The Assemblies of God minister in Fredonia also spent the entire night in prayer. The Church of Christ opened its doors too—and the Baptists and the Methodists. And, thanks to the nurse who had been on the scene, Fr. Steven even found himself on the Mennonite prayer line. Later, he would credit his survival to this outpouring and uniting of these Christian churches in prayer.

And, when he miraculously recovered, things returned almost to normal for a time. Not quite normal, of course: Fr. Steven wore a halo around his head for several months. And no, I don't mean that this halo was a supernatural illumination of his head. Rather, it was a cage of screws attached to and immobilizing his head, much more akin to a crown of thorns than an indication of sanctity. He would wear this for five long months, from December until the following April—and he was grateful that he didn't need surgery after it was removed.

And then, in more or less record time after an accident so severe as his, Fr. Steven was recovered enough to return to his regular duties, and he went back to Sacred Heart parish once more.

One day, shortly after his return, Father was celebrating a regular weekday Mass. One of the readings was from the Gospel of Luke—a reading that Father had heard many times before. It was the account of the tenant farmer giving his fig tree one more chance to bear fruit:

> And he told this parable: "A man had a fig tree planted in
> his vineyard; and he came seeking fruit on it and found
> none. And he said to the vinedresser, 'Lo, these three years

I have come seeking fruit on this fig tree, and I find none. Cut it down; why should it use up the ground?' And he answered him, 'Let it alone, sir, this year also, till I dig about it and put on manure. And if it bears fruit next year, well and good; but if not, you can cut it down.'" (Luke 13:6–9)

The irony of the reading was lost on Fr. Steven. That is, until something started to happen. When Fr. Steven was reading the Gospel from the lectionary, the page itself became suddenly illuminated to his eyes, and then it grew larger and larger. Then, finally, the page actually came out of the lectionary and charged Fr. Steven.

"I'm German," Father says. "Things don't happen like this." And yet it did.

This all happened in front of the congregation. Just a daily-Mass-size crowd, but nevertheless public. It was clear to him that no one else had just seen what he had seen, so he did his best to be calm about it and not disrupt the Mass. He describes acting as though nothing had happened and finishing Mass as best as he could under the circumstances.

Fr. Steven then went back to the rectory, sat down in his chair, and started to think. Several cups of coffee later, he began to remember the events and conversations he had had following his accident. But they were not conversations on the side of a Kansas highway. No—he was not in Kansas anymore.

Before the Judgment Seat

The memories of where he had been and whom he had seen while he was near death suddenly came flooding back to Fr. Steven.

"I was before the Judgment Seat of Jesus Christ," Father begins. He then describes the illumination of conscience: "I have no way of telling how long it lasted. We went through my life entirely. Accusing me of various things, to all of which I said, 'Yes.' There was no rebuttal."

This was the moment. All of us, for whatever reason, know this moment is coming. How we all know it, we can only speculate. Maybe it's our share in human nature, our shared Creator, or just thousands of generations of NDEs and OBEs being told and retold around the campfire. It is much more than just some nebulous speculation. It is a reality.

This moment is so well-defined in our minds that we all plan for it, in one way or another, whether we admit it or not. We all do, and Fr. Steven was no different. But what happened that day was not how Fr. Steven had planned things out in his head:

> Now I had it planned, as I think many of us do, that when I got before his Judgment Seat, I could give a lot of excuses to say, "But Lord, she pushed me that day to the point I couldn't do anything else," or "Lord, I had a bad day, I didn't feel too good you know, and that was the reason why I didn't do this." I had a number of excuses. That was not the case. Everything He said … I was talking to Truth! Truth, and when you're talking to Truth, you can't give excuses. All you say is "Yes, that's the truth." That's all I said, "Yes. That's just, Lord, I know."

Have you ever had this experience, where you walk into a situation ready to defend yourself, but then you get there and all your excuses just suddenly seem to fade away, to evaporate? Maybe you were standing before your parents in judgment. Maybe you were standing before an actual judge in judgment. If our excuses cannot withstand earthly scrutiny, how can we possibly think they will hold up before the Almighty? Divine mercy presumes divine justice.

Given this context, consider the infinite irony of Jesus standing before Pontius Pilate in judgment. How could an earthly judge ever stand before the Divine Judge? And yet what does Pilate say? Standing before Truth itself, Truth incarnate, Pilate says, "*Quid est veritas?*" "What is truth?" Basically, "I don't know what truth is."

There is much truth, even honesty, to Pilate's statement, because it is an affirmation of the fact that Pilate cannot recognize Truth even when He is staring him in the face.

God's presence is such that the truth becomes undeniable. His logic is irrefutable.

Fire Insurance and a Good Confession

Some people have asked Fr. Steven if he knew whether he was in a state of mortal sin before the accident. Perhaps they are of a mind that if a priest is not sure of his own state of moral peril, then they, as laypeople, certainly couldn't be sure either, should they find themselves in a similar situation. And certainly Fr. Steven's experience is supposed to be somewhat scary, but it is important that we experience the right kind of unsettling fear when we look at it and think about how we might apply what he experienced to our own lives.

The devil loves a good distraction, and people could definitely miss the importance of Fr. Steven's message because of a distraction just like this: What if I don't know if I'm in a state of mortal sin? What if Confession did not work because I unknowingly did my part wrong?

Fr. Steven may have had a litany of excuses prepared, but unfortunately, he did, in fact, know that he was living in a state of mortal sin. He knew because, even though he had received the Sacrament of Reconciliation and properly confessed his sins, he did not truly intend to amend his life.

As he says, the Sacrament of Confession was more like "fire insurance": "Appropriate confession means that you change your life, and I wasn't about to change my life. I used that sacrament as fire insurance." And Fr. Steven admitted that that fire-insurance approach did not work. In fact, it utterly failed him.

How should he have approached the Sacrament of Confession? For starters, he should have conducted himself as if Hell really exists and as if his getting to Heaven depended on his making a good confession—contrition and a firm purpose of amendment included.

The Council of Trent defined *contrition* as "sorrow of soul, and a hatred of sin committed, with a firm purpose of not sinning in the future."[121] But Fr. Steven did not have a firm purpose of amendment. He was not putting forth any real effort:

> I have wondered how many of my confessions were valid because I had no firm purpose for amendment. I felt sorry, but the kind of sorrow I had was not really sorrow. [There was] sorrow involved because I knew that if I died with these sins on my soul I was threatened by Almighty God with eternal damnation. That kind of sorrow does not cut the mustard.

Fr. Steven lacked perfect contrition and true sorrow for his sins. If contrition is based on other motives, such as loss of Heaven, fear of Hell, or the weight of guilt, it is termed *imperfect contrition*. Even with imperfect contrition, however, a penitent receives absolution. But if we're just afraid of the earthly consequences, that is neither contrition nor attrition, perfect or imperfect. For example, if I

---

[121] Sess. 14, chap. 4.

have committed a crime, I cannot just be sorry that I'm going to jail in order to really be contrite.

Kids teach us the meaning of true contrition all the time. Is little Billy sorry because his slingshot is being taken away or because he hurt his sister? Just so, because Fr. Steven lacked true sorrow for his sins, he did not have a firm purpose of going and sinning "no more." He was not actively resolving to stop himself and to change his habits.

There's Time!

Fr. Steven was not actively pursuing the path of holiness. He was not entering into the spiritual battle. He was not actively asking Jesus for help in the midst of temptation. He was not imploring the help of the Virgin Mary and the saints or his guardian angel.

Not only that, but Fr. Steven *knew* something was coming. Jesus had warned him, even before his accident. Even with that warning, though, Fr. Steven simply refused to amend his life:

At the time of my almost demise, I was in the unfortunate situation of not caring and taking some things for granted, which I should not have taken for granted, assuming some things that I should not have assumed. There's time, there's time for me later on to convert, become a good priest, to change. There's time. But He was saying, "Steven, there's no time." I had two small accidents; the second one was greater than the first. I told my former pastor I feel that the other one's coming. The next one will be the big one. It was. He had his ways of warning me. I didn't listen. I wouldn't listen. I purposely wouldn't listen because of the pleasure that I was experiencing, and it wasn't about to be taken away from me.

Fr. Steven might not have known all the details of the car accident that was about to happen, but he knew that a critical moment was approaching. He had some kind of premonition. Somehow, he knew his clock was counting down, yet he never truly decided to change his ways. This is a rut that so many of us can fall into.

"There's time!" There's also time to convert, to make necessary changes, to stop sinning—all sometime *later*. What's one more sin? I'll start my diet after one last bite. No doubt most of us have our own version of the weak prayer that St. Augustine once prayed: "Lord, make me chaste—but not yet."

Have you heard the old story about the fence? No one really knows its origin, but it seems to crop up from time to time. This is how it goes.

There was a crowd of people, and a fence ran through the crowd. Jesus stood on one side of the group, and Satan stood on the other. Both Jesus and Satan called to the people in the group. One by one, each made up his or her mind and went either to Jesus or to Satan. This went on for some time. *There was time*—time enough for everybody to make a choice. Soon enough, Jesus had gathered around Himself a group of people from the crowd. So had Satan.

One man, however, did not join either group. He climbed onto the fence and, finding it comfortable enough, decided to stay there. Meanwhile, Jesus' group of people left and disappeared in one direction, and Satan and his group disappeared in the other.

But the man remained on the fence, sitting alone—for a time, that is. After a while, Satan returned. He appeared to be looking for something.

The man, having no one else to talk to, asked Satan, "Have you lost something?"

Satan looked straight at the man on the fence. "No," he answered. "There you are. Come with me."

The man said, "But I sat on the fence. I chose neither you nor Him."

Satan answered, "Fine, but I own the fence."

Fr. Steven's Judgment and Advocate

This is the moment.

Fr. Steven's soul hangs in the balance. Jesus has taken Fr. Steven through his entire life, and he knows the state of his own soul now. In short, he knows that the examination did not go well. Can you imagine how Fr. Steven must be feeling at this moment?

We can each imagine for ourselves how this moment will reverberate, one way or the other. Eternity lies on either side of this judgment. Convicted criminals know this feeling all too well, but a life sentence—even a death sentence—is nothing compared with the sentence each of us will be given for all eternity.

So what judgment did Fr. Steven receive? "At the end, He said my sentence is Hell. Again, I said 'Yes, Lord. I know.' That's the only thing I could have said. That's the only logical thing He could've said. I knew this is what I deserved. I didn't see Him, I just heard."

But that is not all Fr. Steven heard. He then heard the voice of his advocate. Even though the various earthly justice systems are pale comparisons to the Divine Court, apparently they get one thing right: perpetrators have the right to representation. We still receive a representative before the Court of Final Judgment. And if you do not have one of your own, the Court will appoint one for you.

You should get down on your knees right now and pray that, when the time comes, the finest advocate the world has ever known will represent you. Pray that you will have the greatest possible attorney to plead your case. Who is this advocate? Can you guess whose voice Fr. Steven heard?

Then I heard a female voice, "Son, will You please spare his life and his eternal soul?" He said, "Mother, he's been a priest for twelve years for himself and not for me. Let him reap the punishment he deserves." She continued by saying, "But Son, we can give him special graces and strengths and then see if there's fruit. If not, Your will be done." There is a very short pause. [Jesus came] back. He said, "Mother, he's yours." Ever since then, I have been hers.

If Fr. Steven did not already understand why the page of the lectionary flew at him, he did as he remembered this moment. Here was the Gospel parable of the fig tree being given one more year, one more chance, to bear fruit. Only this was the parable of Fr. Steven's life.

This advocate is our Mother. She is Fr. Steven's Mother. These words will hopefully hit you in a deep way. We cannot fall too deeply in love with the Blessed Mother, because we can never love her more than Jesus does. The Virgin Mary advocates and intercedes for us, just as she did at the wedding at Cana. This is the role of the queen of Israel—the *Gebirah* in Hebrew—who intercedes for the people before the king.[122]

Mary especially intercedes for sinners, as she did for Fr. Steven. St. Bonaventure says, "Mary takes care of all, even of sinners."[123] Mary especially glories in being called the "Advocate of sinners," as she once declared to the Ven. Sr. Mary Villani: "After the title

---

[122] See John 2:1–11 for the account of the wedding at Cana and 1 Kings 2:13–22 for the account of Bathsheba, the mother of Solomon, advising Adonijah, "Pray ask King Solomon," and "he will not refuse you."

[123] St. Alphonsus Liguori, *The Glories of Mary* (Redemptorist Fathers, 1931), chap. 2.

of Mother of God, I glory most in being called the Advocate of sinners."[124]

From that day on, Fr. Steven belonged to Mary. He committed himself to a deep, authentic love for the Queen of Heaven, who directly rescued him from eternal damnation. And, in so doing, he was about to become a true priest of God.

Mary, too, has been with him ever since. Of course, she always was, even when he was not particularly aware of her or devoted to her: "There are things that she's told me and done for me that she should not have done and told me. But this is the kind of mother we have. You may be saying, 'But Father, you just had a very special devotion to her before the accident.' No. I have to give another indictment of myself. Just as hard."

But he's a priest, right? How could a priest not believe in the Blessed Mother? But note, Fr. Steven did not say he did not believe in the Blessed Mother before his accident. He simply said he was not *devoted* to her. This difference is huge. It's critical. I knew a wonderful priest, Fr. Marvin Kitten, now deceased—please pray for the repose of his soul—who would often say in spiritual direction, "The longest journey of all is from the head to the heart."

Before Fr. Steven's NDE, he possessed only a superficial or intellectual belief in the Virgin Mary. This limitation of his relationship was not just with Mary, either—Fr. Steven believed in the angels, the saints, and even in Jesus Christ Himself merely in this intellectual way. Though a priest, he still had not made that true conversion of heart.

But who better than our Blessed Mother to soften and turn our hearts to Jesus? Jesus knew this, even from the Cross. That's

[124]St. Alphonsus Liguori, *The Glories of Mary*, chap. 2.

why His last command before He died involved her: "Behold, your mother!" (John 19:27). Fr. Steven comments on this:

> We have a Mother. I didn't have any special devotion to her, but since then—she's become everything. At the foot of the Cross, Jesus looked down upon her and the apostle He loved and said, "Woman, behold, your son," meaning, "Mother, I'll give you the whole Church now as your sons and daughters. They're yours." She takes that very literally, very seriously. So any one of us in the same stead would suffer the same consequences and experience the divine mercy of our Lord Jesus Christ. That's what I experienced: His mercy. But his Mother is the one who came and interceded for me.

Fr. Steven witnessed and benefitted from the full intercessory power of the Queen Mother on display in Heaven.

As was said of the queen mother of Israel, Bathsheba, the king "will not refuse" her. Even King David himself said of his mother, "I cannot refuse you" (1 Kings 2:17, 20).

It is important to recognize that the Blessed Mother's power in Heaven is entirely dependent on Jesus and His love for her. Jesus "cannot refuse" the Blessed Mother out of His special love for her. This is not because the Virgin Mary wields power over Jesus or over God the Father. She is certainly not some sort of supergoddess. She is a queen mother, not a queen who is coequal or superior to the King of Kings. A queen mother's power derives from her son's power.

Bathsheba was merely a foreshadowing, a type, of the Virgin Mary. Can we even fathom the glory of the mother of the King of Kings? After his experience, Fr. Steven shared, "One thing I've learned since then is this beautiful truth—with regard to the Trinity, the Father, the Son, and the Holy Spirit. None of them, not one, can say 'No' to Her. They cannot. It's impossible. They will not say 'No' to her. Isn't that somebody that we want on our side?"

Yes! We want the Virgin Mary on our side. More than that, we want to be her knights and her ladies-in-waiting, for she is our Queen. What's more, the Blessed Virgin Mary is the "safest, easiest, shortest and most perfect way of approaching Jesus."[125] Why? Because Jesus came to us through Mary, so we can go to Him through Mary as well.

That's the short answer. For the long answer, consecrate yourself to the Blessed Mother. St. Louis de Montfort wrote the book on it: *True Devotion to Mary*. All the greatest saints of recent centuries highly recommend this work and his *Total Consecration to Jesus through Mary*.[126]

"We Have Only One Home, and It's Not Here"

Fr. Steven's whole understanding of reality, what was true and what was actually important, changed in this moment. He says, "When I regained the consciousness and the ability to think again, that's one of the things that I was very well aware of—that they are the only real things that exist, that we're the ones that [are] the shadow world. That we have only one home, and it's not here."

---

[125]St. Louis Marie de Montfort, *True Devotion to Mary* (Montfort Missionaries, 1987), par. 55.

[126]The author has published a new translation of St. Louis de Montfort's *Total Consecration to Jesus through Mary*. The translation is faithful to de Montfort, but the language is simpler and easier to understand. *St. Louis de Montfort's Total Consecration to Jesus through Mary: New, Day-by-Day, Easier-to-Read Translation*, trans. Scott L. Smith, Jr. (Holy Water Books, 2019).

This is not our true "home." St. Thérèse de Lisieux is often quoted as saying, "The world's thy ship and not thy home." We need to live like this—this is what Fr. Steven realized. It is so easy to focus on this passing world, a place filled with consumerism and constant noise. Megastores, endless commutes to work, streaming, and binge-watching are all just a mirage, shadows of the realities that lie on the other side of earth. The reality is that there is constant war between Heaven and Hell, angels and demons, raging beyond the veil and influencing everything, but most of the time we can't see it, so we think it doesn't exist. This all changes when God pulls back the curtain and permits an NDE or an OBE. Fr. Steven describes this in terms of priorities:

> [I realized that] a lot of our priorities are mixed up, that my own priorities were mixed up, that my priority should have been to save my soul and help save others, which was what a priest should do anyway. To invest in that future, not in the future that I was vested in of happiness here on earth as a retired priest.

That priority is not just for priests! Saving our souls and the souls of all those around us is our *primary* vocation on this earth. If you're a husband or wife, your job is to get your spouse to Heaven. If you're a mother or father, your job is to get your children to Heaven. No matter your occupation—if you're a butcher, a baker, or a candlestick maker—your most important job is to get everyone you know to Heaven. As they say of the plantation Tara in *Gone with the Wind*, "It's the only thing that matters. It's the only thing that lasts." What we do for Christ's Body, the Church, is all that matters. Everything else turns to dust, and quickly—even Tara. St. Ignatius of Loyola taught this as the First Principle and Foundation, the entire purpose of our creation: "God created human beings to praise, reverence, and serve God, and by doing this, to save their souls."[127]

Beware of Pride

Fr. Steven was somewhat surprised that Jesus did not seem to care what his parishioners thought of him:

One of the things that I was amazed at was that He didn't take … a popularity poll. He knows our hearts. [Jesus is] the only one that matters, as far as I'm concerned, and what anybody thinks of Fr. Steve Scheier doesn't matter. He's the only one that counts. No one else, because I'm alone before Him in judgment. I can't point to anybody else and say, "Oh Lord, she made me do it." He knows. He knows.

As Fr. Steven said, "No one else." What we do for Jesus and in His name is all that matters. Eternity is not decided for us based on some sort of earthly popularity contest. In fact, speaking truth is far more likely to make us unpopular than popular in the ways of the world. But speaking truth is part of what gets us to Heaven—an essential part. When Fr. Steven is asked to give advice to priests, he tells them:

We should not be afraid of telling things like they are, as we see them, as they should be. That's going to make us unpopular, but that's part of being His follower. He never promised that we would be popular for being His follower.

---

[127] St. Ignatius of Loyola, "The First Principle and Foundation," *Spiritual Exercises*, trans. Elder Mullan, S.J., ed. Rick Rossi, March 2015, https://www.bc.edu/content/dam/files/offices/ministry/pdf/First%20Principle%20and%20Foundation%20-March%20 2015%20(2).pdf.

He only promised crosses, but the crosses are bearable because He's there and because His blessed Mother's there, to lighten them.

Isn't it funny how easily we can be lulled into such a false way of thinking, believing that Heaven is the reward for maintaining a good reputation among everybody and offending nobody? Prompting us to desire to be liked and respected is one of the most elegant of the devil's traps, for such things are natural goods, but it is all too easy for the pursuit of them to get out of hand.

When this happens, we find ourselves mired in the sin of pride. Even priests can fall into this deadly sin. And, as many priests will tell you, priests *especially* fall into this sin. They stand in the place of Jesus Himself, after all. They are ordained with real power, natural and supernatural.

We are taught that pride is the original and most deadly of the seven deadly sins. It is also the most clearly demonic because it was the cause of the devil's fall. In pride, we image Lucifer. In humility, we image Jesus.

Because humility is such an important virtue and such an important lesson to be learned from Fr. Steven's experience, the Litany of Humility is a most powerful prayer. For this reason, I have included it in full at the end of this book. Cardinal Rafael Merry del Val (d. 1930) wrote this litany while serving as secretary of state of the Holy See under Pope St. Pius X. It is a prayer that C. S. Lewis, even though he was not Catholic, was known to like.[128] I strongly urge you to make a habit of praying it daily, for the devil does *not* want you to pray for humility.

---

[128] "For the litany composed by Cardinal Merry many thanks." *The Collected Letters of C. S. Lewis*, vol. 2, ed. Walter Hooper (New York: HarperCollins, 2009), 959 and n. 26, ebook.

A Priest for Him

Fr. Steven has talked about the particular susceptibility of priests to the sin of pride. Pride, he says, attacks each of us, but especially priests because of the "prestige of the priesthood":

> When He said that I was a priest for myself and not for Him, that hit [the nail] on the head, because it didn't matter [to me] whether He was involved at all. The prestige of the priesthood, it kept me more in line, so to speak, with my peers. I had no problem in saying Mass, but I had no problem in missing Mass either. None. The Eucharist did not mean as much to me as it did to some priests. I had other priests go on and on about their first Mass. Mine was never that way. I think [it was an] attitude of not being a priest for Him, not being a follower of Him, which means suffering.

This suffering that Fr. Steven describes is the antidote to pride. Pride is a terrible trap, devouring souls. But there's an easy way out—suffering. Pride is like cartoon prison bars—you can walk right through them. If priests embrace suffering, they become priests "for Him." This is true for all of us, if we will embrace redemptive suffering in the Cross of Christ.

Note how Fr. Steven had "no problem missing Mass" and how impoverished his understanding of the Eucharist was! Parishioners tend to love priests with a casual attitude toward mortal sin. It helps them become "one of the guys." But isn't this true of all of us?

Notice also how Fr. Steven's casual attitude corresponded with the lack of an underlying longing to truly experience the Mass—he notes that the desire wasn't there, and he knows that it's a problem, but before his NDE, he didn't have the gumption to do anything about it. Can you imagine working all those years to become a priest, to celebrate your first Mass, and then feeling *nothing*? Likewise, can you imagine a husband and wife feeling nothing on the altar, or even after consummating their marriage as husband and wife?

Why is the savor, the potency, of these moments lost? Why does potency turn to impotence, physical or spiritual? It happens when we fail to embrace the suffering that prepares us for the moment. The transcendent beauty and gift of that moment are usually lost on a married couple if they have not embraced the suffering of chastity prior to marriage. In a similar manner, if a priest has not prepared his body and soul in sacrificial constraint and dedication to the gift of his vocation ahead of his ordination, the celebration of his first Mass will ring somewhat hollow and empty.

Fr. Steven describes his "cowardly" approach to suffering and his inadequate preparation as a seminarian:

> Being a priest for myself … I've always run from the cross, always. I found out since then that if we run from the cross there is a bigger one awaiting us wherever we end up. And they're not hard, they're not long-lasting, they're not eternal. And He's always there to make them as sweet as He possibly can, but I was a coward those twelve years. I was a priest who had little training in the spirituality of the seminary life even though I had been in the seminary after eighth grade, you know, twelve years, but there was no spirituality involved. Not like there is these days in some seminaries.

As Fr. Steven says, Jesus is "always there to make [our crosses] as sweet as He possibly can." Suffering is sweet because Jesus is with us in our suffering, and being with Jesus is the sweetest thing of all. Closeness to Jesus is the experience of Heaven itself.

St. Teresa of Calcutta articulates this best in her characteristically simple and nurturing way: "Suffering, pain, sorrow, humiliation, feelings of loneliness, are nothing but the kiss of Jesus, a sign that you have come so close that he can kiss you."[129]

Hell Is for Real: Reasons for Damnation

But Fr. Steven was not just in real danger of being damned because he was living as "a priest for myself" instead of a priest for Christ. He was also worthy of damnation for violating the commandments.

> The priesthood, the life of priests, that's what [Jesus] said, was the icing on top of the cake. The cake was rotten. The icing was bad, bitter. Those twelve years, I pantomimed being a priest.... Everything had to come back to me to give me self-assurance. My homilies, the life that I led in the parish, and the people's comments, all served to uplift me. If I wasn't uplifted, I wasn't doing one of the sacraments. But there were ways to take care of that. We all have ways to escape pain, and I took ways of my own to escape that pain. Priests are as liable to sinfulness as anybody else. And my mission is to let you know, to let priests know, that we are liable to Hell and that Hell exists. But also His Divine Mercy exists. His love outweighs justice.

This image of a rotten cake and bitter icing is as fitting for the priesthood as it is for any other vocation. Am I a good parent if I show up just for the sweet moments in my kids' lives—for instance, when they are all nestled in their beds—but check out when one

---

[129]Mother Teresa, *Mother Teresa: No Greater Love*, ed. Thomas Moore (Novato, CA: New World Library, 1997), 137.

of them has a bad dream or wets the bed or when the baby needs a fifth diaper change in the same night? Am I a good husband if I try to "escape that pain" of my marriage by working long hours away from home, or through excessive alcohol, or by indulging in sexual fantasies?

Fr. Steven's recitation of what led him to damnation can serve us as we examine our own consciences. And on that note, let me emphasize that one critical item for an effective examination of conscience—one I often confess to failing in—is fidelity to prayer time: setting aside time *daily* for prayer. That's another one we will not be able to blame on anyone else. Don't start blaming now.

"A Priest without Prayer Is Dead"

Though Fr. Steven never spoke publicly about what specific sins led to his damnation, he did divulge the following about his prayer life.

Another priest reached out to him and asked whether Fr. Steven was faithful to praying the Divine Office. Maybe you have heard of Lauds, Vespers, and Compline, also known as Morning, Evening, and Night Prayer, respectively? My wife especially loves Compline, or Night Prayer. Together with other prayers that are meant to be prayed at specific hours of each day, these are collectively called the Divine Office or the Liturgy of the Hours.

Prayerfully consider adding one of these to your daily prayer routine. There is a prayer period for every "watch" of the day, or every three hours. This is a continuation of the Jewish Temple liturgy of praying the psalms at these same intervals—this is why Jesus cries aloud from the Cross at 3:00 p.m. the opening of Psalm 22, "*Eli, Eli, lama sabachthani?*"—"My God, my God, why hast thou forsaken me?" (Matt. 27:46). This is also how the Church answers St. Paul's call to "pray constantly" (1 Thess. 5:16–18).

Praying the Divine Office can be a bit daunting at first. There are a couple of apps and websites that are a great help—and just remember to "be not afraid" of all of those bookmarks![130]

Praying the Office is a great option for laypeople. Priests, however, are required to pray it every day. Fr. Steven admitted that he didn't pray the Office faithfully before his NDE. "As we say, a priest without prayer is dead. A priest without the Blessed Sacrament is dead. A priest without the Blessed Mother is dead. I learned my lesson, but it took Him breaking my neck and the threat of eternal damnation just to get my attention."

Fr. Steven makes three "deadly" statements: A priest is dead without (1) prayer, (2) the Blessed Sacrament, and (3) the Blessed Mother. Not only is a *priest* dead without these things—so are we.

Fr. Steven's deadly language might seem a little extreme at first. Remember, though, this man *did* die *and* was sentenced to damnation. It's so important that we remember this powerful perspective. The particular judgment that he faced and *failed* is real. Heaven is for real—and Hell is for real too.

We have to keep eternity ever before us—even though the whole world is trying to distract us from it—or we will die an eternal death.

What Happened to Fr. Steven after His NDE?

Fr. Steven went on to his reward for a second and final time on April 16, 2020. His death occurred right in the midst of the Covid-19 pandemic and the Kansas governor's shelter-in-place proclamation.

The bishop of Wichita, Kansas, Carl A. Kemme, celebrated Fr. Steven's funeral Mass in the Cathedral of the Immaculate Conception. Again, the Blessed Mother was beside Fr. Steven.

---

[130] Universalis.com is both an app and a website. iBreviary.org is another great option. The priests I know tend to prefer iBreviary.

Bishop Kemme said of Fr. Steven, whose suffering became intense in his later years and months, "He nevertheless spent his days in prayer and praise, offering his own pain, suffering, and distress for the glory of God and for the salvation of souls."[131]

The bishop also noted Fr. Steven's transformation following his NDE: "Father Scheier, and all those who lived their lives as he did, now know the source of that divine burning fire. And one day we will as well, when we and all the saints will be consumed by the divine light and live forever in its brilliant glow."[132]

In his concluding remarks, the bishop prayed for Fr. Steven as he faced judgment—something Fr. Steven was blessed to be approaching not for the first time, but for the second time. "We pray that the judge of the living and the dead will look upon Fr. Scheier with mercy and tenderness and invite him to take his place in the new creation."[133]

Let us echo this prayer. And let us also pray that people will live their lives in view of this reality.

Thinking about Eternity

Eternity is a lot to think about. Fr. Steven's experience, though, helps us to grapple with it. More importantly, though, it helps us to *live* with the idea of it.

I will leave you with Mother Angelica's thoughts on the importance of Fr. Steven's experience, when she introduced him to the world on her show: "You hear people say, 'Oh, I wish I were never born.' What a horrible thing to say! You know, even if our life was

---

[131] Catholic Diocese of Wichita, "Father Scheier Passes Away April 16," April 20, 2020, https://catholicdioceseofwichita.org/father-scheier-passes-away-april-16/.

[132] "Father Scheier Passes Away."

[133] "Father Scheier Passes Away."

or is miserable, it is nothing compared with eternity. We're going forward to live with God forever and ever. It's hard to remember or even to think of what it means to live forever."[134]

Forever is quite a lot, but what does *forever* even mean? It is not an easy concept to grasp. And yet we can approach an understanding of it. Aristotle argues that our ability to conceive of such things—namely, concepts such as *forever*, *infinity*, and *eternity*—tells us something about the nature of our rational souls: It tells us that our souls are immortal.

Mother Angelica, in an effort to help us grasp the concept of *forever*, went on to relate a sort of parable she once heard: "Imagine the world as a giant iron ball. Every thousand years a bird comes and sharpens its beak on that ball, and when that is worn down to nothing, that's a moment of eternity."

With that image in mind, Mother Angelica concludes, "We don't want to give it up too easily. We certainly don't want to waste it."

The point of Fr. Steven's experience—of any NDE—is to help us keep this in mind. Keep eternity in mind. Live as though forever hangs in the balance—not just for you, but for your loved ones as well. Because it does.

---

[134] *Mother Angelica Live.*

10

KEVIN WELLS

Kevin Wells's story involves a lot of violence — and blood. And in many ways, it's quite different from the other stories I've told in this book. Perhaps you know about Kevin from his blockbuster book, *The Priests We Need to Save the Church*, from his work with various diocese and seminaries, from his collaborations with EWTN — or even from, a bit more on the nose, his book about his NDE, *Burst: A Story of God's Grace When Life Falls Apart*. Because of what happened to him, he went from being a baseball journalist to dedicating his life's work to God.

An Attack on Uncle Tommy

Kevin's story begins with his uncle Tommy, who was better known to the world as Msgr. Thomas Wells. In Kevin's description of him, he seems like a great, smiling, booming bear of a man, possessed of a "radiant, mocking manner" with "blue Irish eyes, which spoke paragraphs before he ever opened his mouth" — eyes that cut right through you.[135]

He was the kind of priest who sent truckloads of vocations to the seminary, the kind who cut right to the heart of whatever matter

---

[135] Kevin Wells, *The Priests We Need to Save the Church* (Manchester, NH: Sophia Institute Press, 2019), 1.

you were talking about. In just a sentence or two, he could bring you right to the dusty doorstep of Golgotha and start unpacking the mystery of the Cross.

He was the kind of priest who, in authentic consolation, could tell suffering newlyweds and still-childless not-so-newlyweds that "infertility was the complete measure of God's love being poured into them." And he could warn them with sobriety and kindness that trying to solve such a heartache by means of in vitro fertilization was tantamount to saying yes to the ancient dragon.

He was the kind of priest who could melt the ice of cynicism and get you to trust—*really* trust—in God, the kind who never twisted doctrine "in the name of pastoral sensitivity." He was the kind of priest, as Wells has so well argued in his book that I mentioned above, whom we need to save the Church. He was also the kind of priest whom we can scarcely afford to lose—something Satan knew too well.

So when Kevin's mom answered the phone one morning and was told what had happened to her brother, she crumpled under the weight of the news. Reporters thundered into quiet Germantown, Maryland, and into Msgr. Wells's home, Mother Seton Parish.

The fanged serpent—a man with a knife, a homeless drifter, a guy named Robert Paul Lucas—had uncoiled from the local bar, high on cocaine and alcohol, squeezed through an open window in the rectory, and stabbed Monsignor Wells dozens of times.

Kevin Wells would later describe all those stab wounds as being "like stigmata from hell."[136]

---

[136] Kevin Wells, "The Priest Who Resisted Homosexuality in the Priesthood and Died for It," *Crisis Magazine*, June 8, 2022.

"Lucas was a weak man—but it was among the most brutal and violent murder scenes I've been involved with," said one of the lawyers on the case, Deputy State Attorney Kay Winfree. "I always thought there was something in Lucas' past that led him to act with that magnitude of violence."[137] And she was right. The past was definitely rearing its ugly head on that night.

Although the state asked for the maximum sentence of seventy years of incarceration for murder in the first degree, Lucas would go on to only get forty-two years for *second*-degree murder. It was said that the judge felt sympathy for Lucas, given that he lacked any prior record and because a psychiatrist testified that Lucas was "severely traumatized and damaged from a horrible childhood and adolescence."[138]

Despite the judge's ruling, there was no mistaking Monsignor's gruesome death for a mere unfortunate accident.

"Though the killing was of Satan," Kevin Wells wrote, "the circumstances surrounding it hold as much demonic weight. Homosexually active, credibly-accused priests resided in the rectory for many years prior to my uncle's arrival." The same rectory that had become the site of Monsignor's murder had previously "been the site of years of appalling sacrilege and sin."[139]

A Secret Service agent, who had been a close friend and confidant of Msgr. Wells, had a theory about Monsignor's death that aligned with the rectory's history: "I have no doubt about it—that night, his murderer was looking for a 'trick.'"[140]

---

[137] Wells, "Priest Who Resisted."
[138] Sonia Boin Montgomery, "Priest Killer Sentenced to 42 Years," *Frederick (MD) News-Post*, August 14, 2001.
[139] Wells, "Priest Who Resisted."
[140] Wells, "Priest Who Resisted."

After the Murder

A life like Monsignor's, cut short by a death like that, touched thousands of people, inspiring them to a pursuit of virtue in honor of his memory.

But not everyone. After his uncle's devastating murder, Kevin had moved in the opposite direction. He had become a spiritual absentee, practicing a mere pew-warmer brand of Catholicism. He described how he had "allowed a dissolution of standards into my life; I saw where unchecked pride, restlessness, and sloth had closed off any real opening to grow into a mature Catholic adult and a devoted husband and father."[141]

Uncle Tommy's last words to Kevin and his wife had been about embracing their cross, and although this would in time come to completely change the trajectory of their marriage, Kevin shared that "I still too often carried [my cross] like a toddler moaning over a splinter."

Kevin was attending his annual silent retreat at a Jesuit retreat house in Washington, D.C., when he became aware of just how tepid his faith had grown. He was out walking at night, and around midnight, he dropped to his knees on a "graying, gap-tooth-planked dock on the banks of the Potomac River, mere steps from where John Wilkes Booth had hidden on the night he gunned down Abraham Lincoln."[142]

And then he heard the voice of what he knew to be the Holy Spirit: "Die to yourself, Kevin." In this moment of spiritual clarity, Kevin asked for something new, something that it had never occurred to him to ask for before. He later said that his response

---

[141] Wells, *Priests We Need,* 14.
[142] Wells, *Priests We Need,* 13.

to the Holy Spirit's urgings came like a "spiritual bolt of lightning" and, leaning on his baseball background, described it as though it were coming "out of left field."[143]

For some reason, he knew at that moment that he needed and wanted to draw closer to the Sacred Heart of Jesus—a Heart that he knew has been the victim, like his uncle, of so much violence. So that's what he did. Strange as it sounds, he asked God for "violence." And what happened? As soon as he made the request, he was filled with an overwhelming peace.

But a month later, almost to the exact second, that violence he had asked for came smashing down. Kevin would later describe the pain descending on him as though it were a tomahawk flung into the back of his head.

Near Death

Kevin's brain had hemorrhaged because of an aneurysm, and the flow of blood quickly filled his skull. The pressure was incredible. The horrible pain felt like it was splitting his skull apart—and it lasted not for hours or even days, but a week. He was stuck in an unending haze of hallucinations and torture.

Over the course of this horrific week, the doctors tried repeatedly to put shunts in place to manage the damaging cerebral blood flow and to relieve the pressure on Kevin's brain, but they couldn't get it under control—and he was no help. During the intense hallucinations that were caused by his brain injury, he kept imagining that the various medical tubing keeping him alive was clouds of late summer mosquitos. He tore it out repeatedly, jeopardizing and reversing the critical work of the medical team that was struggling to keep him alive.

[143] Personal interview with the author, July 24, 2023.

Meanwhile, even if the shunts were fully functioning, they were just a half measure, redirecting the flow of blood but not sealing it off where it needed to be stopped. And if the aneurysm could not seal itself off, then brain surgery, *deep* brain surgery, would be required. The aneurysm was not in an easily accessible part of the brain; Kevin's chief neurosurgeon referred to attempting such a surgery as the "dark alley" that he hoped to avoid.[144]

One night that week, as Kevin was placed in the tight confines of an MRI machine, in what felt to him like a white plastic coffin, he began choking on his own vomit. But because of his condition, he couldn't move. He couldn't speak. He couldn't scream for help. He realized that he was choking to death while the hospital staff and nurses were just on the other side of the glass, unable to see that he needed help. He knew that, if he could speak a single word, an army of helpers would descend upon him, "yet he opened not his mouth; like a lamb that is led to the slaughter" (Isa. 53:7). He knew he was feeling the same torment felt by the Sacred Heart of Jesus, who suffered silently on the Cross, while surrounded by the vast choirs of angels who would have swooped in to save Him, if only He would have spoken His Word for them to do so.

But in the midst of this panic, Kevin also had perfect clarity of thought. *So, this is what it feels like to die,* he thought. *This is Your plan for my end.*

A Demonic Presence

Standing by during that whole week of Kevin's struggle, the hospital chaplain, Fr. Bill, had a sense that this was more than a "simple" aneurysm. It seemed to him that there was some spiritual and supernatural dimension to the battle that was raging for Kevin's life,

---

[144] Wells, *Priests We Need*, 18.

some unearthly reason why, for so many days, his blood was not clotting where it should have. He even went so far as to tell Kevin's wife, Krista, that "a demonic presence had taken up residence" in Kevin's room. And, in fact, this was not news to Krista, who had never left Kevin's side in his hospital room. She, like Fr. Bill, was also acutely aware of this dark presence.

In Fr. Bill, God had provided Kevin and Krista with a priest chaplain who actually believed in the daily reality of spiritual warfare. This was a miracle in and of itself, as this element of reality has been so often neglected in the last several decades, even by priests. That Fr. Bill believed in the reality of the devil and demons—that he did not view Satan as merely a "symbolic reality"[145] or fictitious personification of social evil or some other dangerous falsehood—*and* that Fr. Bill had personal experience fighting such evil, was a rare combination indeed. Because of this experience, Fr. Bill quickly diagnosed the underlying source of the problem: He sensed the demonic oppression in Kevin's room right away.

In *An Exorcist Tells His Story*, the late Fr. Gabriele Amorth, renowned chief exorcist of Rome, identified the following kinds of *extraordinary* demonic activity, as opposed to *ordinary*, daily demonic temptation.[146]

First, Fr. Amorth describes "external physical pain caused by Satan." We have seen examples of this in the saints who are known to have endured being "pummeled" by demons, such as St. Padre Pio, St. Paul of the Cross, and St. John Vianney. But, although

---

[145] See "Jesuit Superior General: Satan Is a 'Symbolic Reality,'" Catholic News Agency, August 21, 2019, https://www.catholicnewsagency.com/news/42075/jesuit-superior-general-satan-is-a-symbolic-reality.

[146] Father Gabriele Amorth, *An Exorcist Tells His Story*, trans. Nicoletta V. MacKenzie (San Francisco: Ignatius Press, 1999), 32–35.

he was certainly struggling with a severe physical ailment, this is *not* the kind of demonic activity that was affecting Kevin Wells.

Fr. Amorth goes on to describe the kinds of demonic attacks that tend to be more spiritual in nature rather than the physical beatings and abuse in the external attacks described above. These less tangible attacks are the big three that require the involvement of exorcists. They are demonic possession, oppression, and obsession.[147]

Demonic possession is "the gravest and most spectacular form of demonic afflictions." Luckily, Kevin was not possessed. His situation could have been much worse! Likewise, he was not suffering obsession. Rather, he was being oppressed. Job's boils and tragedies are a biblical example of demonic oppression. Job was not possessed, but through demonic attack, he lost his children, his goods, and his health. The "thorn" in St. Paul's side is another example of oppression. In 2 Corinthians 12:7, St. Paul wrote: "And to keep me from being too elated by the abundance of revelations, a thorn was given me in the flesh, a messenger of Satan, to harass me."

Fr. Amorth further explains that demonic oppression is a relatively common occurrence compared with demonic possession:

There is no doubting the evil origin of the affliction. While possessions are still relatively rare today, we exorcists run into a great number of people who have been struck by the devil in their health, jobs, or relationships. We must make it clear that to diagnose and heal an oppression-related illness

---

[147]The remaining kinds of demonic attacks are infestation and subjugation or dependence. Infestation involves a demonic presence attaching to an object or a house, like a haunted house. Subjugation involves a person willingly subjecting, consecrating, or covenanting himself to or with a particular demon or Satan himself. Bad idea!

is not any easier than to diagnose and cure a person afflicted by full possession. The degree of gravity may be different, but the difficulty of the diagnosis and the amount of time involved in healing are the same.

As Fr. Amorth describes and as Kevin's aneurysm demonstrates, oppression-related illnesses can be difficult to diagnose, much less cure. So how did Fr. Bill confront this demonic attack when he witnessed and came to understand just what was happening to Kevin?

First, Fr. Bill equipped Krista with a consecrated Host in a golden pyx. He told her to hold the Eucharist over her husband "to scatter the oppression." He also told her to pray continually for the safety of Kevin's soul and for St. Michael's intercession. Holding the Eucharist in its pyx, Krista kept her arms outstretched over her husband as the invisible battle waged on for his soul, even as Moses had done while the Israelites under Joshua fought the Amalekite army—and even as the Sacred Heart was supported by Jesus' outstretched arms on the Cross.

The Dark Alley

Although Fr. Bill's prayers and his instructions to Krista to rely on the Eucharist as she fought for her husband may have helped stall the advance of the demonic oppression, Kevin's blood flow continued.

Eventually Kevin's medical team attempted a series of catheter embolizations to make the bleeding stop, but these also failed. And now angiograms had revealed a nest of blood vessels releasing blood into the deep recesses of Kevin's brain. At this point, his neurosurgeon realized that the time had come and that there was no other way. It was time to go down the "dark alley" that he had been trying to avoid at all costs: surgery, deep into Kevin's brain.

He began by cutting away a section of Kevin's skull, opening up the back of his head to get clear access so he could make an attempt to untangle the arteriovenous malformation (AVM). But already he realized that the surgery would be a failure. The malformation had been too deep, and once he got in there, he realized that what he had feared was true: He simply could not get the access he needed to resolve the issue. He told Krista that, had he pushed any farther into the cerebellum, he would have killed Kevin.

The fact that he had, for the moment, saved his life, was not much solace to anyone, however. The doctors did not expect Kevin to live longer than a day or two following his failed surgery. Closing him up was tantamount to only a minor delay of his death sentence.

Kevin faced his last day. He had spoken only a few words prior to the failed surgery, and those were all garbled. And now he was no longer able to speak. He was conscious only on the barest of levels, and he could not see or hear. All moments of clarity in the fight were behind him now, and he was down that dark alley. But he was not alone.

"Stackman"

It was time to call a priest for the Last Rites. It was not Fr. Bill who answered that call, however. It was another priest. And would you know it? That other priest just so happened to have been Uncle Tommy's best friend: Fr. Jim Stack. To Uncle Tommy, he had always been "Stackman."

His parish was not far from the hospital, only an hour away. In what turned out to be a providential movement, he had recently felt called to start a healing ministry. It would soon be evident that God had been preparing this moment for Kevin—and for everyone involved.

Fr. Stack was an old powerlifter and a blue-collar priest. He was the perfect priest for his home parish of St. Jerome, which was full of other blue collars and flannel shirts in working-class Maryland. It was the kind of place where "Bruce Springsteen could cut a double album."[148]

Together, Uncle Tommy and Stackman had been a beloved pair of priests. They were funny and streetwise, but they didn't falter in the face of hardship or moral dilemmas. They stood their ground when assaulted by the opportunities of pandemic sins, and they encouraged the parishioners in their flocks to do the same. They were fighters, at once battle-hardened and tender, ruthless and winking, and "hyperaware that grave, stampeding sin puts us on a downward spiral to Hell."

Hell was well aware of these two priests' potency. Ever greedy, it had tried to take them both down at once: one from murder, the other from despair. Fr. Stack's dad had died just days before Uncle Tommy's murder, and he wasn't coping well. After burying his best friend and his dad in quick succession, Fr. Stack tried burying himself too—in his work and pastoral demands. Lost in spiritual desolation, he was harassed constantly by temptations, doubts, and lies—and he was slowly becoming convinced that he was a bad priest and had lost his faith.

"I was in bad shape for a very long time. I couldn't feel His presence," Stack said. "And then Satan came to smash and crush my faith. I just didn't want to believe anymore. I went numb. The whole world was continuing, but I was just standing at the bus stop, trying to find a way."

---

[148] Kevin Wells, *Burst: A Story of God's Grace When Life Falls Apart* (Cincinnati: Servant Books, 2011), 118.

But Heaven was busy writing straight with crooked lines. According to Fr. Stack, "Then I went on a retreat, and everything changed."[149] That was when he had a moment of personal revelation in which the Holy Spirit had told him he needed to start a healing ministry—but he was not too keen on the idea.

"Embarrassing stuff," Fr. Stack called it. He thought people "would think [he] was some kind of kook." As Kevin described it, Fr. Stack "kicked off his healing ministry with all the eagerness of a kindergartner in line for a flu shot."[150]

Even so, he did not ignore his call entirely. He just tiptoed his way through it. He healed in secret. He was afraid his colleagues would see him as some kind of snake-handling Pentecostal. Even his own parishioners were unaware of his healing ministry.

Though this work freed him from the depths of the wasteland he'd been suffocating in, Stackman hobbled along in this hidden fashion for years. That is, until he traveled to Mexico in 2007 on a pilgrimage to the Basilica of Our Lady of Guadalupe.

On one beautiful golden morning of his pilgrimage, Fr. Stack decided it was time to climb Tepeyac Hill, where the Blessed Mother had appeared to Juan Diego in 1531. As he approached the summit, Fr. Stack was suddenly overwhelmed by tears of "humiliation and dread." And he heard a voice too. This was now the second time he had heard this voice, and again, he felt himself convicted by the Holy Spirit.

"But it was different this time. All of a sudden there was a loud inner voice that clearly said to me, 'You're grieving me! I'm ashamed of you! I gave you this gift of healing, and you're not using it. I need you to heal now. If not, I'll take it away.'"[151]

---

[149] Wells, *Burst*, 121.
[150] Wells, *Burst*, 122.
[151] Wells, *Burst*, 123.

Stackman had not even reached the summit of Tepeyac yet. When he did, there was another voice waiting for him. But Mary's voice was gentle: "Do not be afraid. If you entrust your ministry to me, I will take care of you. Let me take care of the Holy Spirit."[152]

"It was those words that finally empowered me," Fr. Stack said. Quackery, kooks, and snake-handling be damned; Stackman was on a mission.[153]

When he got home, his parishioners saw that there was suddenly a new item in the parish bulletin: "Healing Mass. Sunday, 4:00 p.m." And with that, Fr. Stack assembled a team and dove, all reservations overcome, into this brave new ministry. The healings and miracles started flowing. And just in time too—because Msgr. Wells's nephew was suddenly in need of a healing miracle. A big one.

Kevin's Unique NDE

As Fr. Stack and his healing-ministry assistant arrived at the hospital, they had both just finished praying the Chaplet of Divine Mercy: "O Blood and Water, which gushed forth from the Heart of Jesus as a fountain of Mercy for us, I trust in You!" Then, together, they entered the dark room where Kevin was lying comatose.

Fr. Stack's assistant was Mary Pat Donoghue, an impressive individual in her own right. She was the principal of what had been his parish's failing school, but she rescued St. Jerome Academy, transforming it with the principles of a Catholic liberal education, as detailed in Rod Dreher's 2017 book, *The Benedict Option*. She

---

[152] Wells, *Burst*, 123.
[153] Wells, *Burst*, 123.

now serves as the executive director of the Secretariat of Catholic Education for the U.S. Conference of Catholic Bishops.[154]

In their prayers for Kevin, Fr. Stack and Mary Pat had been calling on all their local saints, the saints of Maryland, Baltimore, and the Washington, D.C., area. These included Mother Mary Lange,[155] St. John Neumann, and St. Elizabeth Ann Seton. As Fr. Stack began the Anointing, they continued to call on these local saints.

Ever since the conclusion of the failed surgery, Kevin had been unresponsive. Nevertheless, Fr. Stack leaned down and asked him a question, whispering in his ear, "What saint do you want to intercede for you?"

Fr. Stack was stunned, first, that Kevin responded. But even more surprising was the person he asked for: "Bring my uncle down," Kevin had whispered. "I need Tommy now."

Those were Kevin's first words that day, his first words since the failed surgery. And, strangely, he has no memory of saying anything. Despite all outward appearances and throughout all that followed, Kevin never actually regained consciousness at that point.

But Stackman didn't hesitate to do as he was told, and he called on his old friend. "Hey, Tommy. Hey, buddy," he begged. "Kevin needs you now. He's calling for you to save his life."

At these words, they saw a "benevolent fire" suddenly fill the room, descending as if from Heaven. Unlike most of the other NDEs and OBEs we've looked at in this book, the individual who

---

[154] Zoe Romanowsky, "Veteran Educator Outlines Her Vision for Reinvigorating US Catholic Schools," *National Catholic Register*, August 22, 2023, https://www.ncregister.com/interview/veteran-educator -outlines-her-vision-for-reinvigorating-us-catholic-schools.

[155] Now Venerable Mary Elizabeth Lange.

was near death was barely aware of what was happening around him. Instead, it was the people next to him who witnessed the miraculous occurrence. Neither Fr. Stack nor Mary Pat had any explanation for what was happening. It was clearly supernatural. They wavered a bit on their feet and almost joined Kevin in unconsciousness. Despite being an old brawler and just having had a mystical experience in Guadalupe, Stackman recalled nearly fainting.

"There were lights everywhere," he told Kevin later. "Everything in [the] room took on light. And all of a sudden, the presence of Tommy and the saints surrounded your bed, and everything took on a great warmth. I felt the whole heavenly court around [you]. It was overwhelming."[156]

Mary Pat was standing beside Fr. Stack during all this. She experienced a "powerful, pleasant pulsing, like a warm electric current, that moved through her whole body."[157]

"The whole room got really warm, and I began to feel dizzy," Mary Pat described. "I've been assisting Fr. Stack for a while now, but I've never felt what I felt in that room."

Kevin remembers very little from that event. As mentioned, he does not remember calling for his uncle Tommy. He does, however, remember a "sustained, palpable warmth coursing through his chest and abdomen." Kevin said the following: "The heat seemed to settle deep within me. It was like the warmth that gently wrapped around me as a child when I sat on the stone hearth of my grandparents' fireplace after coming in from a Pennsylvania winter night."

Uncle Tommy, along with a beaming retinue of local saints and the throngs of Heaven, crowded into Kevin's hospital room that

---

[156] Wells, *Burst*, 125.
[157] Wells, *Burst*, 125.

night. Stackman stood at the center of these multitudes, continuing to anoint Kevin's broken head and to pray, as the lights and luminaries swirled around him.

And Uncle Tommy? He did what he was invoked to do. The next day, they received the results of a new angiogram: The AVM had vanished. The errant blood flow had stopped. The trapped blood and fluids had vanished. And Kevin realized that the pain was almost gone.

Kevin's head was healed, but the doctors were all mystified. The violence God had allowed had run its course, and the demonic oppression had been exorcised by the combined strength of the full heavenly court.

After Fr. Stack left that night, two of Kevin's friends witnessed one last flickering light. Again, Kevin has no memory of this, but they told him later that he suddenly raised his arm and pointed to the corner of his hospital room. "Look," he whispered. "It's the Lady of Guadalupe."[158]

And there she was. It makes one wonder if she hadn't been there all along.

[158] Well, *Burst*, 126.

CONCLUSION

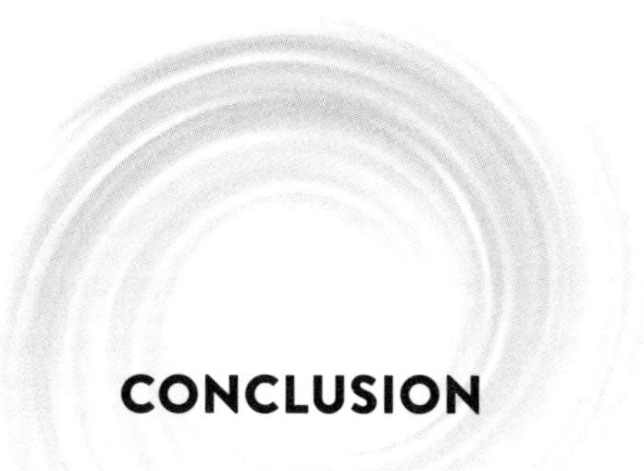

Near-death experiences are usually treated as contemporary oc-currences. But this is an explicitly *Catholic* examination of them, and the Church is ancient. In a certain sense, the Church has been present for all time. Therefore, it is not surprising that we have found not just ancient accounts of NDEs, but testimonies scattered throughout history.

When I began this undertaking, I did not think to expect this. Now, at the conclusion (or at least the first conclusion), I realize this is exactly the case. One can find Catholic accounts of Heaven, Hell, and Purgatory throughout history.

In addition to the relatively few accounts I shared in detail in this book, I uncovered in my research compelling and consis-tent accounts of NDEs in nearly every century of the Church's last two millennia — and even in pre-Christian history, in the Old Testament.

I analyzed many contemporary and twentieth-century accounts of NDEs as well, including that of layman Kevin Wells, which I shared in our last chapter. Another account that, due to space considerations, I did not include in detail here but that I encourage you to look up is that of Sondra Abrahams. She is a laywoman who experienced a striking NDE some decades ago and has provided a number of video interviews sharing what happened.

And, of course, I have also shared with you some of the stories of contemporary priests who have seen such things: Frs. Steven Scheier and Cedric Pisegna.

We have looked at more recent saints, such as Padre Pio, and we have also analyzed nineteenth-century accounts, such as that of St. Thérèse of Lisieux. We have studied medieval and Renaissance accounts of NDEs and OBEs, such as that of St. Teresa of Ávila. We have studied the sixth-century accounts provided by Pope St. Gregory the Great, and the NDEs and OBEs of the apostolic and biblical ages through Sts. Paul and John, as well as through Jonah.

We have thus met the goal of our inquiry, a comprehensive review of specifically *Catholic* NDEs and OBEs. What should be obvious to us now, however, is this: We're just getting started. Catholic iterations of such experiences can be found, if analyzed in this new light, everywhere in salvation history. This is just the beginning, because God is the beginning and the end, the Alpha and the Omega. No NDE or OBE, no words that we use to describe them—and no poet who tries to do it for us—can adequately describe what awaits us on the other side of the veil.

LITANY OF HUMILITY

O Jesus, meek and humble of heart, *hear me.*

From the desire of being esteemed, *deliver me, O Jesus.*

From the desire of being loved, *deliver me, O Jesus.*

From the desire of being extolled, *deliver me, O Jesus.*

From the desire of being honored, *deliver me, O Jesus.*

From the desire of being praised, *deliver me, O Jesus.*

From the desire of being preferred to others, *deliver me, O Jesus.*

From the desire of being consulted, *deliver me, O Jesus.*

From the desire of being approved, *deliver me, O Jesus.*

From the fear of being humiliated, *deliver me, O Jesus.*

From the fear of being despised, *deliver me, O Jesus.*

From the fear of suffering rebukes, *deliver me, O Jesus.*

From the fear of being calumniated, *deliver me, O Jesus.*

From the fear of being forgotten, *deliver me, O Jesus.*

From the fear of being ridiculed, *deliver me, O Jesus.*

From the fear of being wronged, *deliver me, O Jesus.*

From the fear of being suspected, *deliver me, O Jesus.*

That others may be loved more than I, *Jesus, grant me the grace to desire it.*

That others may be esteemed more than I, *Jesus, grant me the grace to desire it.*

That, in the opinion of the world, others may increase
and I may decrease, *Jesus, grant me the grace to desire it.*
That others may be chosen and I set aside, *Jesus, grant me
the grace to desire it.*
That others may be praised and I go unnoticed, *Jesus,
grant me the grace to desire it.*
That others may be preferred to me in everything, *Jesus,
grant me the grace to desire it.*
That others may become holier than I, provided that I
may become as holy as I should, *Jesus, grant me the
grace to desire it.*[159]

---

[159] Merry Cardinal del Val, "Litany of Humility," from the prayer book
for Jesuits, published by the Eternal Word Television Network.

ABOUT THE AUTHOR

Scott Smith is a Catholic author, attorney, and theologian. He and his wife, Ashton, are the parents of six wild-eyed children, thirteenth- and fourteenth-generation, respectively, Catholic residents of Pointe Coupee Parish, Louisiana.

His other books on theology and the Catholic Faith include *Consecration to St. Joseph for Children & Families*, which he co-authored with Fr. Donald Calloway; *Lord of the Rings & The Eucharist*; a new translation of St. Louis de Montfort's *Total Consecration to Jesus through Mary*; *The Theology of Sci-Fi: The Christian's Guide to the Galaxy*; *Pray the Rosary with Saint John Paul II*; *The Catholic ManBook*; and *Everything You Need to Know about Mary but Were Never Taught*. His fiction includes *The Seventh Word*, a pro-life horror novel, and the *Cajun Zombie Chronicles*, the Catholic version of the zombie apocalypse.

Scott is undertaking a massive project of Catholic conversions, called "The 8 Million," with His Eminence, Cardinal Raymond Burke. The goal is eight million Catholic conversions, like those that followed the apparitions of Our Lady of Guadalupe in 1531, leading up to the five hundredth anniversary of Our Lady of Guadalupe in 2031 and the two thousandth anniversary of redemption and Pentecost in 2033. Let's give the Blessed Mother a bouquet of eight million souls as an anniversary gift for her Son!

Scott regularly contributes to his blog, *The Scott Smith Blog*, at www.thescottsmithblog.com and is the co-host of several podcasts, the *Catholic Nerds Podcast*, *Dad Monk*, and *Saints by Number with J Zumo*.

Sophia Institute

Sophia Institute is a nonprofit institution that seeks to nurture the spiritual, moral, and cultural life of souls and to spread the gospel of Christ in conformity with the authentic teachings of the Roman Catholic Church.

Sophia Institute Press fulfills this mission by offering translations, reprints, and new publications that afford readers a rich source of the enduring wisdom of mankind.

Sophia Institute also operates the popular online resource CatholicExchange.com. *Catholic Exchange* provides world news from a Catholic perspective as well as daily devotionals and articles that will help readers to grow in holiness and live a life consistent with the teachings of the Church.

In 2013, Sophia Institute launched Sophia Institute for Teachers to renew and rebuild Catholic culture through service to Catholic education. With the goal of nurturing the spiritual, moral, and cultural life of souls, and an abiding respect for the role and work of teachers, we strive to provide materials and programs that are at once enlightening to the mind and ennobling to the heart; faithful and complete, as well as useful and practical.

Sophia Institute gratefully recognizes the Solidarity Association for preserving and encouraging the growth of our apostolate over the course of many years. Without their generous and timely support, this book would not be in your hands.

www.SophiaInstitute.com
www.CatholicExchange.com
www.SophiaInstituteforTeachers.org

Sophia Institute Press® is a registered trademark of Sophia Institute.
Sophia Institute is a tax-exempt institution as defined by the
Internal Revenue Code, Section 501(c)(3). Tax ID 22-2548708.